2 3 4 **5** 6 7 8 9 10

THE TECH SET

Ellyssa Kroski, Series Editor

W9-BXN-945

Wikis for Libraries

Lauren Pressley

lita

Neal-Schuman Publishers, Inc.

New York   London

Published by Neal-Schuman Publishers, Inc.
100 William St., Suite 2004
New York, NY 10038

Published in cooperation with the Library Information and Technology Association, a division of the American Library Association.

Copyright © 2010 Neal-Schuman Publishers, Inc.

All rights reserved. Reproduction of this book, in whole or in part, without written permission of the publisher, is prohibited.

Figures 1.3, 2.1, 3.3–3.5, 3.8, 3.12–3.13, and 3.17 appear courtesy of PBWorks (http://pbworks.com).

Printed and bound in the United States of America.

The paper used in this publication meets the minimum requirements of American National Standard for Information Sciences—Permanence of Paper for Printed Library Materials, ANSI Z39.48-1992.

ISBN: 978-1-55570-710-1

To my husband, John Borwick,
who first introduced me to wikis way back in 2002
and has continued making my world
a bigger and more interesting place every day since then.
Thank you for being such an amazingly supportive partner in all things.

CONTENTS

Don't miss this book's companion wiki and podcast!

Turn the page for details.

THE TECH SET is more than the book you're holding!

All 10 titles in THE TECH SET series feature three components:

1. the book you're now holding;
2. companion wikis to provide even more details on the topic and keep our coverage of this topic up-to-date; and
3. author podcasts that will extend your knowledge and let you get to know the author even better.

The companion wikis and podcasts can be found at:

techset.wetpaint.com

At **techset.wetpaint.com** you'll be able to go far beyond the printed pages you're now holding and:

- ▶ access regular updates from each author that are packed with new advice and recommended resources;
- ▶ use the wiki's forum to interact, ask questions, and share advice with the authors and your LIS peers; and
- ▶ hear these gurus' own words when you listen to THE TECH SET podcasts.

To receive regular updates about TECH SET technologies and authors, sign up for THE TECH SET Facebook page (**facebook.com/nealschumanpub**) and Twitter (**twitter.com/nealschumanpub**).

For more information on THE TECH SET series and the individual titles, visit **www.neal-schuman.com/techset**.

FOREWORD

Welcome to volume 5 of The Tech Set.

Wikis for Libraries is a comprehensive guide to harnessing the power of the wiki as a collaboration tool, content management solution, and reference resource. Readers will learn how to leverage the potential of wikis to create internal knowledge bases and intranets within their organizations, facilitate collaboration among diverse team members, design library instruction tools, support special events, and create valuable online resources. Author Lauren Pressley deftly conveys the process of how to create a wiki and transform it into a "living" resource that will continue to evolve with your organization. Everything from planning and choosing a software product to extending your wiki through widgets can be found in this all-in-one manual.

The idea for The Tech Set book series developed because I perceived a need for a set of practical guidebooks for using today's cutting-edge technologies specifically within libraries. When I give talks and teach courses, what I hear most from librarians who are interested in implementing these new tools in their organizations are questions on how exactly to go about doing it. A lot has been written about the benefits of these new 2.0 social media tools, and at this point librarians are intrigued but they oftentimes don't know where to start.

I envisioned a series of books that would offer accessible, practical information and would encapsulate the spirit of a 23 Things program but go a step further—to teach librarians not only how to use these programs as individual users but also how to plan and implement particular types of library services using them. I thought it was important to discuss the entire life cycle of these initiatives, including everything from what it takes to plan, strategize, and gain buy-in, to how to develop and implement, to how to market and measure the success of these projects. I also wanted them to incorporate a broad range of project ideas and instructions.

Each of the ten books in The Tech Set series was written with this format in mind. Throughout the series, the "Implementation" chapters, chock-full of detailed project instructions, will be of major interest to all readers. These chapters start off with a basic "recipe" for how to effectively use the technology in a library, and then build on that foundation to offer more and more advanced project ideas. I believe that readers of all levels of expertise will find something useful here as the proposed projects and initiatives run the gamut from the basic to the cutting-edge.

There's a reason Lauren Pressley was named a Library Journal Mover and Shaker in 2009—she's a creative innovator who "walks the walk." And her knowledge and experience shine through in *Wikis for Libraries*, which leads readers through the entire process of creating and using one of these social media tools. Library wiki enthusiasts will want to keep this volume at hand for both ideas and techniques.

Ellyssa Kroski
Information Services Technologist
Barnard College Library
www.ellyssakroski.com
http://oedb.org/blogs/ilibrarian
ellyssakroski@yahoo.com

Ellyssa Kroski is an Information Services Technologist at Barnard College as well as a writer, educator, and international conference speaker. She is an adjunct faculty member at Long Island University, Pratt Institute, and San Jose State University where she teaches LIS students about emerging technologies. Her book *Web 2.0 for Librarians and Information Professionals* was published in February 2008, and she is the creator and Series Editor for The Tech Set 10-volume book series. She blogs at iLibrarian and writes a column called "Stacking the Tech" for *Library Journal*'s Academic Newswire.

PREFACE

In an age when libraries must provide users with up-to-the-minute information, wikis are a powerful tool for collaboration and communication. If you're stuck wondering "What is a wiki?", then you are already behind in providing the latest in Web 2.0 customer service. Wikis are at the forefront of ways in which libraries are communicating with staff, patrons, and other libraries.

Wikis are nothing more than really easy-to-edit Web sites. In fact, many Web sites run on wiki software, though the average user would not identify them as a wiki because using the software doesn't mean they have to look like Wikipedia. The wiki's strength is that a user can change the content displayed on the page just by clicking an "edit" button on that page. Even those who tend to resist technology can learn to edit a wiki page. This is a radical shift from the early days of the Internet, when only coders and computer experts had the ability to alter content on the Web. Today anyone can do it. Wiki Web sites make use of various levels of access and privacy, allowing one person, a select group of people, or everyone to contribute to or edit an organization's Web site without needing to know HTML or how to FTP to the Web site server. Wikis using a WYSIWYG editor are so easy to use that everyone in your organization can participate, and the simplicity of the technology means staff can use their time for more creative purposes.

Wikis for Libraries walks you through the step-by-step process of implementing library wikis, from the initial stages of planning through to marketing, and then measuring their overall effectiveness. Every library operates under a different set of circumstances with varying financial and technical resources, and this book discusses the various options, from free and simple-to-use solutions to solutions that require extra financial and technical resources, so that all librarians can take advantage of this versatile and valuable tool.

▶ ORGANIZATION AND AUDIENCE

This book can be read from start to finish or used as a reference to quickly find solutions to specific problems, depending on your background and experience with wikis. If you are just getting started, you will probably want to turn to Chapter 1 to get background information about wikis. If you are already using a wiki in your workplace, you may want to turn to the sections on marketing, best practices, and assessment.

Chapter 1 introduces wikis, highlights their benefits for library service, and provides screenshots to demonstrate features all wikis have in common. Chapter 2 explains the different types of wikis that libraries implement, steps for planning a wiki, and types of software needed to run a wiki. Chapter 3 unveils a step-by-step process you can use to quickly launch a basic wiki. It also covers locally hosted versus vendor hosted wikis, as well as internal versus external use of wikis in libraries. Chapter 4 discusses how to market your wiki, from programming to social media. Chapter 5 showcases best library practices, and Chapter 6 details the metrics of how to assess the usefulness of your wiki in meeting your community's information needs.

As you may have deduced by its name, Wikipedia is a wiki. However, Wikipedia is just one example of an active wiki. Because most people will be familiar with Wikipedia, I use this site for illustrative purposes throughout this book. Please realize that other wikis exist, and there is a good chance that you regularly visit wiki-based Web sites without even realizing it.

Wikis for Libraries is designed for all information professionals. Whether you work in an academic library, a school media center, a public library, or a special library, the pages that follow are aimed at you and your services. Library staff in public services and youth services and those in behind-the-scenes technical support roles can all find ways to use wikis for better communication, awareness, and information service.

I hope after reading this book you will use wikis for content management, reference information, and collaboration. With a little creativity, and following the steps in this book, you can establish a wiki that will help you bring your library to the forefront of Web communication.

ACKNOWLEDGMENTS

Part of what makes this field so remarkable is the extended library community of people interested in exploring new Web 2.0 tools and technologies. I am grateful to be part of a community of library bloggers and Twitterers who come together to discuss emerging technology and its potential impact on our field.

Writing this book has been a commitment in both time and energy. In particular I would like to thank John, Mom, Dad, Katherine, and my family for their support along the way.

I would also like to thank my library's visionary dean, Lynn Sutton, who embraced wikis early on, and my innovative supervisors, Susan Smith and Erik Mitchell, who are always willing to give something new a try. Thank you to Kaeley McMahan, Kevin Gilbertson, and Elizabeth Novicki, who are constantly ready for a discussion on the future of the field. I would also like to thank Giz Womack, Roz Tedford, and Tim Mitchell, who are always willing to chat about technology. Thank you to Mary Scanlon, Sarah Jeong, Mary Lib Slate, Ellen Daugman, Bobbie Collins, and my colleagues at the Z. Smith Reynolds Library for their continued support.

I would like to especially thank Ellyssa Kroski for the opportunity to participate in this project and for her insightful comments and conversation along the way.

►1

INTRODUCTION: WIKI BASICS

- ► **Definition and Evolution**
- ► **Benefits of Wikis**
- ► **Elements of a Wiki**
- ► **Wiki Culture**

► DEFINITION AND EVOLUTION

Wikis are essentially Web sites that are really easy to manipulate. You have used a wiki if you have visited Wikipedia. There is also a good chance that you have used other wikis and not known it. Many Web sites use a wiki to put Web content online but don't explicitly market their site as a wiki. This is part of what makes wikis a useful tool: they can be used for anything from a site created to publish information for others to a collaborative and interactive Web site designed with user participation in mind.

The word "wiki" comes from the name of the first wiki Web site. It was named the "WikiWikiWeb" after the Hawaiian term "wikiwiki," which means "very quick" (*Oxford English Dictionary*, 2007, http:// dictionary.oed.com). This nomenclature is appropriate because the nature of wikis is not only that they are easy to create, but they are quick to contribute to and edit, as well. In fact, for most wikis editing is as easy as clicking an edit button, modifying the existing information, and clicking "Save."

Today, wikis are used in a number of ways: as stand-alone Web sites, as "live" reference resources, as supplemental information (like for this book), or as community collaboration spaces.

The first Web site to refer to itself as a wiki was the WikiWikiWeb. This site was released in 1995. Soon after this there were other wiki Web sites. These sites were primarily used by programmers but grew in scope and topic. Wikis became known to a larger world of users with the introduction of Wikipedia in 2001. According to Alexa (www.alexa.com/topsites), a Web information company, the interactive encyclopedia's growth has steadily increased. Today, Wikipedia ranks in the top ten most visited Web sites. Wikipedia serves as an excellent example of a wiki. As with any wiki, Wikipedia is a Web site composed of linked pages. Its content is a collaborative effort, which anyone can edit. There is little organization, and most content is found through searching the entire Web site.

Librarians have had a contentious relationship with Wikipedia for some time. The very nature of the site—unclear authority, fluidity in content, no prepublication vetting—means the source lacks key features librarians look for in quality information. However, countless articles have been written about Wikipedia's credibility, and some librarians are beginning to embrace Wikipedia, if not for the content, then for the fact that it provides solid bibliographies on a number of topics and good outlines to help broaden and narrow a topic. The very characteristics that have caused librarians to avoid Wikipedia can be useful when teaching library instruction sessions. Pointing out issues such as lack of authority, official editing processes, and possible biases in Wikipedia can lead to dynamic class discussions about the importance of these characteristics in any resource.

It is possible that library staff might be hesitant to incorporate wikis into their technology toolkit if they have been wary of Wikipedia. If your library staff is predisposed to avoid Wikipedia and make a case against it, it might be necessary to focus on education and thoroughly plan your implementation before discussing the use of a wiki for your community.

Although librarians might not have always liked Wikipedia, some librarians have appreciated a use for wikis from their earliest days. Librarians have used wikis to create handbooks, research guides, training modules, and Web sites. These librarians do not necessarily know computer languages or have time for tedious

Web site editing, but they have made use of the benefits of this type of tool from its earliest days. Sometimes wikis are used for Web sites created for external audiences. Other times, wikis are used to create intranets for internal use only.

As wikis become increasingly part of the mainstream Internet, many librarians are becoming more comfortable with them, Wikipedia included. Although there are no concrete numbers, it is clear that wikis are becoming part of the common toolkit that libraries use to better serve their users. The Library 2.0 movement encouraged this adoption, and certain providers, such as PBworks, have specifically designed their wikis to meet the library demand driven by this trend. The American Library Association offers wikis for committees, divisions, and other ALA groups. A number of individuals and other library groups have created wikis to help library staff share tips and tricks from their organization with the larger library community. Increasingly the question is not if a library uses a wiki, but how it got started using them and what the library uses a wiki to accomplish. This book is designed to help people starting at this point. But first, let us take a look at the elements of a wiki.

▶ BENEFITS OF WIKIS

Wikis have a number of potential benefits, which is why so many libraries and other organizations have adopted them. Here are some of the primary reasons people choose to implement wikis:

- ▶ Ease of Web site creation
- ▶ Ease of adding and editing content on the Web
- ▶ Capability of adding information to the Internet without knowing HTML
- ▶ Ability to see the revisions of a document over time
- ▶ Distinct space for the content as well as a space for discussion about the content
- ▶ Ease of sharing files with a number of people

One question that people frequently face is when to use a wiki versus another type of technology, such as a blog. In order to make a decision, first you need a clear understanding of what your goal is for your project. Once you understand your needs, you'll know what features you need, and once you have this list you will be in a good position to select a tool.

For example, if you want a way to share news and recent events with your community, you might select a blog. If you need a way to make short announcements quickly, you might select a micro-blogging service like Twitter. However, if you're looking for a way to easily make a Web site, and you want the Web site to function as a portal, a reference resource, or a collaborative workspace, a wiki will meet your needs best.

▶ ELEMENTS OF A WIKI

Although wikis vary depending on the software that runs them, there are a number of features that you can expect to find in nearly any wiki-based Web site. Figure 1.1 shows a screenshot of a handbook created for student assistants at the Z. Smith Reynolds Library of Wake Forest University. The screenshot is of a MediaWiki Web site and contains features specific to wikis running that software platform as an example of the typical layout and navigation of a specific type of wiki. Although not every type of wiki shares the same layout or organization, there are trends among wiki platforms. For example, the "Article," "Discussion," "Edit," and "History" tabs you see across the top of the page in this example could be included as a sidebar in another type of wiki. The links in the sidebar of this wiki could be located elsewhere on the page. This Student Assistants wiki migrated across several different wiki Web sites and had a different layout and design on each platform, before finding its permanent home as a MediaWiki Web site stored on a library server. Although the site changed each time it migrated to another platform, some features were present in every version of the wiki: an overall wiki title, editing and other site page tabs, and a sidebar (see Figure 1.1).

▶ Figure 1.1: Structural Elements of a Wiki

Every wiki will have a **title**. This is the name of the wiki site. Although the portion of the wiki shown in Figure 1.1 is about microforms work, the content is part of the broader Student Assistants wiki. The wiki title refers to that broad topic.

As wikis are editable Web sites, most will provide **tabs** or links that will let users edit the wiki and give them a place to discuss the wiki content before editing and to see previous revisions of the wiki content. These features give wikis their core strengths: the ability to edit, negotiate content, and see how the information on the Web site evolves. The History feature also allows editors to revert to a previous version of the wiki if something accidentally happened to the content or if it has been vandalized.

Finally, there are a number of useful links that are located in the **sidebar** of a wiki. Users can search the wiki for specific information, log in to edit the content, and use a variety of wiki tools, depending on the wiki software's options.

In addition to this basic structure of a wiki, a number of other features are also consistently part of specific pages within a wiki. The pages within a wiki contain the content of the wiki. This is where wiki editors add content for others to read or where they go to collaborate on projects. Library employees collaborated on creating the Student Assistants content (see Figure 1.2), and student assistants read the content and use the wiki as a reference source.

Each page within a wiki has its own **page title**. This is different from the wiki title as it describes the specific content on a given page. The majority of the information on a wiki page is the **content**. This is where editors add the information they wish to include in the wiki and is what people visit the wiki to see. Wiki editors may choose to include text, charts, or multimedia on their wiki pages.

Some wikis allow users to upload **images** and **videos** to the wiki, where they can be saved and viewed. Other times, wikis allow users to embed images and videos from other sites, using the "embed" code that can be found on YouTube and Flickr pages. Wikis that allow you to embed images and videos often also allow you to embed other Web site widgets, extending the functionality of your wiki. Other wikis have built-in modules to ease the process of adding other types of content. These modules allow you to click a box to select the pieces of information you would like to include in your wiki.

▶ Figure 1.2: Content Elements of Wiki

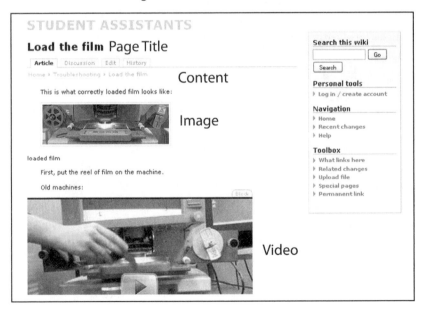

Figure 1.3 shows a screenshot from a collaborative wiki created by library workers from a number of organizations. These librarians use their Library Day in the Life wiki to link to blog posts describing the daily work they do. This resource was created to share information with other library staff members as well as potential library workers. The wiki is hosted by PBworks, a Web-based wiki provider. This type of wiki provides a WYSIWYG, or "What You See Is What You Get," editor. This means that as you edit the wiki, the text displays as it will when you publish the page. Instead of learning a special syntax to write for the wiki, you can use the buttons at the top of the page as you might in a word processing program.

The edit **tab** allows you to change the **content** on the page. The editing interface for any wiki page will display the current page content as well as allow editors to make changes and additions to the existing information. The editing side of the wiki parallels the read-only side. The key features that exist in most wiki editing platforms include buttons to **format** and **save** the content and a text box for the wiki content. Editors can save and see previews of the content before publishing. Wikis also provide a way to format text,

▶ Figure 1.3: Editing Wiki Content

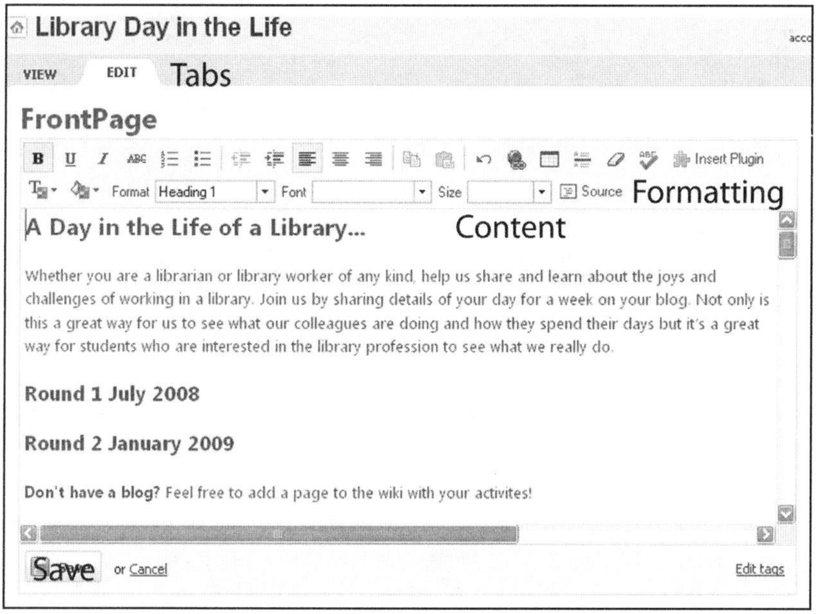

either through the use of wiki markup syntax or through a formatting toolbar that is familiar to users who have used word processing programs. Some wikis give editors the ability to provide a summary of their changes for the benefit of other users who may want more information about the changes.

These are the basic features of wikis, their content, and the editing side, no matter if the site is a MediaWiki installation on a local server or if it is a freely hosted PBworks wiki on the Internet. The exact layout and descriptors might be different, but the basic idea remains true across most wikis. You should be able to click an "Edit" link to edit a page, make changes, and save them. In many of these cases you should be able to see the history of the page as well.

▶ WIKI CULTURE

Now that you have a background in the evolution of wiki use and the basic ways that editors can interact with a wiki site, let's take a look at the controversy that has surrounded Wikipedia. As a popular and controversial Web site, Wikipedia provides us with a familiar example of some of the objections people might raise to a wiki-based site. Wikipedia also is an excellent example of how some of the features that could concern some users can also be the strengths that make the Web site a productive and useful one.

One of the key criticisms of Wikipedia is that there is a lack of authority in each article. It is rarely clear exactly who edits what page, and, in most cases, the pages have several authors. This lack of authority increases the difficulty in judging the quality of the content on any given page. In addition, as multiple people edit every page, the pages are fairly fluid. Someone adds content to a page, and a few minutes later someone else could edit his or her additions. Citations typically point to a fixed work so that researchers can follow up on the original research. Wiki pages are never fixed, so the only way to cite a specific work is to include the exact moment in time in which you accessed the page. Finally, there is no governing body checking the accuracy of any of the content in Wikipedia. There are general rules for contribution, but they rely on the volunteer community of editors to enforce it. Occasionally, when there is sufficient controversy, specific pages will be locked down to minimize vandalism. But there is no final editor checking content for accuracy and style.

For obvious reasons you can see why librarians and educators have been hesitant to encourage the use of Wikipedia and why some teachers do not allow students to use it in their homework. However, even with all these flaws, Wikipedia ends up being a fairly reliable resource. In 2005, Giles reported in *Nature* (available at www.nature.com/nature/journal/v438/n7070/full/438900a.html) that Wikipedia was approximately as accurate as *Encyclopedia Britannica.*

Today many Wikipedia articles are very good. In fact, savvy users can identify the editors with a strong reputation to help identify which articles to trust. Users can look for locked articles to see where a controversy might surround a topic. They can check the "Discussion" tab to see what people have argued about in the content of the article and what is generally agreed upon. Regardless of the quality of the article, the references that follow can lead users to more reliable articles elsewhere on the Internet. The table of contents for Wikipedia articles can help students broaden or narrow a research topic. The links within articles can help users find related keywords for library database or catalog searches.

Librarians can help their users by teaching them to acknowledge Wikipedia as a first step in research. Helping students and community members learn that Wikipedia can give them a general understanding of a topic, which will help them as they progress through the research process, is a way of acknowledging that the source is a useful one. It also points out that the library has additional information that will make their research stronger.

In other words, the key is to realize that Wikipedia is a fundamentally different type of reference source. You cannot trust that the content is reliable because of the credibility of the author or publisher or that an editor oversaw the resource. You have to use a few more information literacy skills, new strategies, and a critical eye when deciding if the material is relevant for your work. These approaches are growing in importance with Web 2.0 sources of information and the emergence of online self-publishing, so they are useful skills to develop.

In realizing that wikis are a different type of resource, and being aware of some of the concerns people raise, you have a good perspective from which to think about how you will use a wiki in your own work. If you want your wiki to be authoritative, you might choose to have only a few specific people edit it. For example, if you want your wiki to explain how the library works, you can limit the editors to the library staff only. If you want to make sure that the content is consistent, you can have guidelines for contribution so that the wiki does not change that often or so that when it does you note recent changes or have a "Last Updated" link to let users know what changes have occurred. However, if you want the site to be a collaborative one that is open to everyone, you can plan to put strategies in place first. You can create policies that people must follow to participate in the wiki, you can monitor changes to make sure nothing is vandalized, or you could simply put a disclaimer on the front page letting people know that the site is open and regularly changes. Thinking through the concerns people might have with a wiki site, and how you will respond to them, before you begin will help you avoid controversial issues or problems in your own wiki Web site.

If you are using a wiki as a workspace, or if you are creating a community-created Web site, you might want to start your wiki using more traditional rules and norms, such as open access to content, limited rules about content and editing, and inclusion of community-driven content. Creating strict guidelines for contribution will increase the challenge in encouraging a wide use of the tool. You will need to give up some control if you want the community to contribute and feel ownership.

Wikis, as prime examples of Web 2.0 participatory culture, tend toward more flexible rules for participation. This flexibility is what gives them strength. This is a shift in thinking that has challenged some traditional approaches in the way we work and have inspired countless blog posts, articles, and, recently, several books.

If this topic is interesting to you, please see the Recommended Reading list at the end of this book for more information.

Giving your community an opportunity to contribute offers them more ownership of the organization, promotes an interest in what your organization is doing, and creates an atmosphere in which they are *part* of the library rather than just *users* of the library. To get started, let's take a look at the different types of wikis you will consider when starting a wiki Web site.

▶2

PLANNING

- ▶ Determine the Purpose of Your Wiki
- ▶ Choose Your Wiki Software
- ▶ Assess Staff and User Skills
- ▶ Get Staff Buy-In

▶ DETERMINE THE PURPOSE OF YOUR WIKI

A successful wiki requires a strong plan for implementation. Determining the purpose of your wiki, the strengths and weaknesses of different software options, and the skills and financial situation of your library will help you identify the variables that will affect your decisions about the type of wiki you choose to implement.

Content Management

One of the most basic ways you can choose to make a Web site is by using a wiki. Once you install a wiki and have added the appropriate logos and style to it, you can enable other people within your organization to add content to the pages. The library staff will know the Web site is a wiki, but your users will just see it as a Web site.

Libraries that choose a wiki platform for their Web site do so because it allows multiple content creators to have access to the Web site so that they can add their own information without having to go through a gatekeeper. It is an efficient way for a reference librarian and a children's librarian both to manage their appropriate sections of the library Web site without having to depend on a

Examples of Wiki Use in Libraries

Content Management	University of Minnesota Libraries Staff Wiki	https://wiki.lib.umn.edu
	University of South Carolina Aiken's Gregg Graniteville Library	http://library.usca.edu/
Collaborative Workspace	Durham County Library Strategic Plan	http://dclstrategicplan.pbworks.com
	Library Information and Technology Association's BIGWIG	http://wikis.ala.org/lita/index.php/BIGWIG
Reference Resource	Albany County Public Library Staff Wiki	http://albystaff.pbworks.com
Training Guide	Z. Smith Reynolds Library	http://wiki.zsr.wfu.edu/studentassistants/

Webmaster. This gives library staff more authority over their work while freeing up Webmasters to spend their time on other responsibilities.

Collaborative Workspace

Wikis can also provide a collaborative workspace. In this sense the look of the wiki does not really matter, The important aspect is that the wiki is located in a place where everyone can access, contribute, and edit content. These collaborative workspaces can be for a library staff, for an association committee, or for a community of librarians spanning the country. A wiki can be project based, or it can be a community-driven reference resource. A wiki can also provide space for collaboratively writing an article or planning a presentation.

Those who use wikis as collaborative workspaces use the sites as a space for a number of people to add and edit content as well as multimedia. This allows the group to collaborate without sending numerous e-mails back and forth, and it saves the group from having to keep multiple files organized and up-to-date. When thinking about using a wiki as a collaborative workspace, keep in mind that you can easily set privacy and control settings to allow only specified people to see and edit the content.

Reference Resource

Wikis excel as a reference source. Wikipedia is a good example of this. Library wikis can be used in the same way: as a reference source for patrons on local history, detailing library policy, or any other topic that the library staff can authoritatively address. Some use wikis to create research guides on subjects of interest for their community. Wikis can also be created specifically for library staff, students, and volunteers as an internal resource to help them to know what they need to know for their job.

As many people are already used to using Wikipedia as a reference source, it is not a stretch to teach them to use another wiki as another type of reference source. Building on the strength of the software and users' expectations, reference wikis are easy to explain to patrons and easy for them to use.

Training Guide

Along the same lines, wikis can be used to create training guides for staff, students, and adult learners. Using the internally linking pages, a wiki can contain a linear path that users must take to get the information they need in the order in which they need it. The benefit of using a wiki to do this is that it can both be a handbook and a reference source for staff. Within the reference Web site you can add modules for staff and students to work through in order to come away with the required skill set.

▶ CHOOSE YOUR WIKI SOFTWARE

Once you have decided to use a wiki for your library, you will need to decide which wiki software to use. Your decision will be based on all the same factors you considered when you were thinking about using a wiki: the skill set that you or your library staff has, the amount of time you want to invest in setting up the wiki, the amount of customization you want to be able to do, as well as the financial resources you would like to devote to the project. Knowing as much as you can about your library's technical capabilities, financial abilities, workload, and desired wiki features will give you a strong background from which to consider different wiki software packages. Involving your technology staff in this process from the very beginning is a good idea as well. They know the most about your library's technology infrastructure and can help you understand what the options are earlier in the decision-making process. Knowing as much as possible about your own position will situate you to make the best decision for your library.

Locally Hosted vs. Vendor Hosted

The first decision you need to make is if you want someone else to host your wiki for you or if you want to host the wiki yourself. This means that you have to decide if you want to go to a wiki Web site and create your own account and wiki there or if you want to install it on your own server space.

Hosting a wiki on another Web site has some clear benefits. The barrier to entry is lower. You do not have to know the technical side of things—you just need to know how to set up an account and click "Save." Because the process is simple and does not require technical staff, it can be easier and faster to get the wiki started. Most hosting sites will back up your content for you, giving you one less thing to worry about. Many vendor hosted wikis also are set up to be especially easy to use. Editing windows will likely use a WYSIWYG editor, making editing more like contributing to a Word document than something technical. Many make the process of hosting files easy by allowing you to put a document in one place for several people to access. Vendor hosted options can be particularly useful for a proof-of-concept example or a pilot program.

However, there are drawbacks to vendor hosted options. It can be difficult in the future to migrate content between a vendor hosted option and an installed, or locally hosted, option if you do not plan ahead. When you host a wiki yourself, you do have to have a skilled staff and sufficient time, as well as your own server space to host the wiki. If you have all of these and choose to host your own wiki, you will be able to have a much higher level of customiz-

Pros and Cons of Locally vs. Vendor Hosted Wikis

Locally hosted wiki:

PROS

> ▶ Wiki can be customized as much as your technical staff is able
> ▶ Your organization has access to the content and can archive as you wish
> ▶ The ability to host means you have access to any wiki platforms and can make your decision based on your specific needs
> ▶ Access may be limited using more sophisticated tools such as LDAP

CONS

> ▶ Requires more staff time and technical skills
> ▶ Requires server space
> ▶ Must create plans for archiving and backing up content
> ▶ May require more support and training as people learn to edit the wiki

Vendor hosted wiki:

PROS

> ▶ Can create a pilot wiki without requiring support from technical staff
> ▶ Can go live quickly and easily
> ▶ No technical knowledge required
> ▶ Vendor takes care of backing up content
> ▶ Editing interface tends to be fairly simple
> ▶ Training is simple

CONS

> ▶ Fees may be associated with a vendor hosted wiki
> ▶ Advertisements might display on your wiki
> ▶ Aesthetic customization may be limited
> ▶ If the vendor goes out of business, you may find yourself manually converting content for your next wiki platform

ation. You can put the wiki at the URL of your choosing, you can change the look of the wiki as much as you would like, and you can control the data. One library issue of particular relevance today is ownership and preservation of digital content. When you host a wiki yourself, you can back up, preserve, archive, and ensure the content will continue to be available into the future.

Some libraries might not be able to use vendor hosted wikis. Some school libraries have blocks and filters that limit Internet access, and wiki sites sometimes fall into the category of Web sites that are blocked. If this is the case, your only option might be a locally hosted wiki. In this case, you would need to pay careful attention to privacy settings to ensure an environment appropriate to your institution. If you do not have the technical skill or access to servers, you will need to see if someone in IT can install and set up the wiki for you. In some cases, the IT department or school administration might decide that a wiki is not appropriate for the institution. If your library has a filtered Internet connection, it would be wise to talk with the administration to determine if a wiki is worth pursuing before investing time in planning and the creation of content.

Vendor Hosted Solutions

If you are looking for a vendor hosted wiki that is easy to use and is frequently used among libraries, consider PBworks (http:// pbworks.com). PBworks was designed with ease in mind. PBworks sites are quick to set up and easy to work with. One of their target audiences is the education market, and many libraries make use of their product. Figure 2.1 shows the start screen for a new PBworks wiki. Note the clearly marked links in the sidebar for creating new pages, uploading files, sharing specific wiki pages, and organizing the wiki content. PBworks pages also allow for community comments, a feature that is particularly useful if the wiki is designed to be a collaborative and interactive Web site.

Another easy-to-use wiki platform is Wetpaint (www.wetpaint .com). This prevalent wiki service makes it easy to create a Web site for free using a wiki format. Although Wetpaint's emphasis is on creating a Web site, their wikis can still function as a collaborative space for a committee or group to work together. Figure 2.2 shows

▶ Figure 2.1: PBworks Wiki Start Page

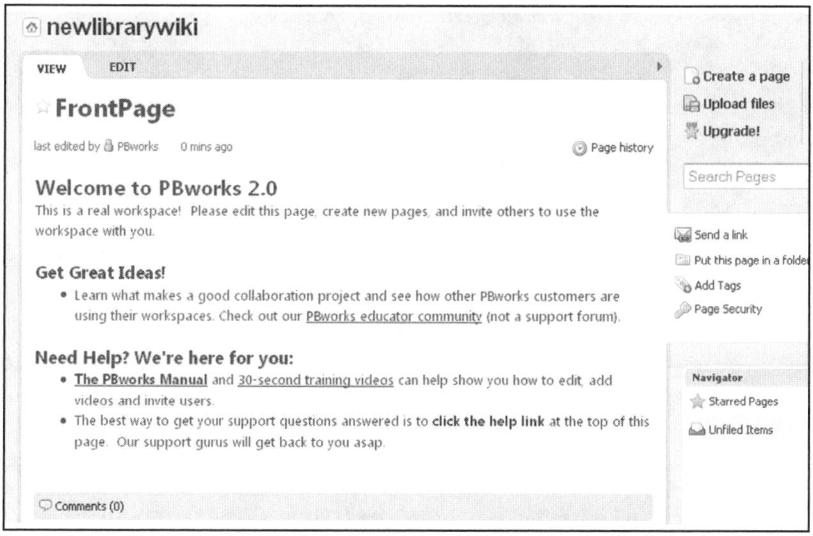

▶ Figure 2.2: Wetpaint Wiki Start Page

a new Wetpaint wiki start page. The buttons across the top of the wiki page make it quick and easy to add new pages, photos, and videos, which help make these sites dynamic and engaging.

Wikispaces (www.wikispaces.com), like PBworks, targets the education market as one of their core audiences. They emphasize that their editing interface is particularly intuitive. Figure 2.3 shows the first page of a new Wikispaces wiki. You can see that the

▶ Figure 2.3: Wikispaces Start Page

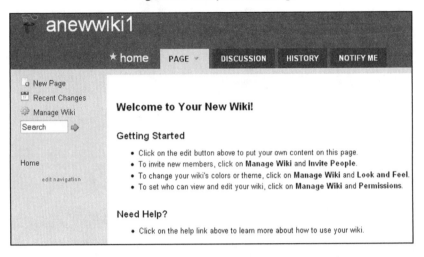

clean design is easy to navigate and that the "Discussion" and "History" tabs are easy to locate. If you are using a wiki for an information literacy class, Wikispaces has the added benefit of emphasizing the process of knowledge creation. The use of the "Discussion" and "History" tabs can be part of the course work and can help students reflect on the process of creating knowledge and publishing.

There are other vendor hosted wikis, for example Wikia (www .wikia.com), from which to choose. With any hosted option, you will have a free (or trial) version that you can use to get started. You can choose to start with the upgrade version if you think the service is worth it or if you need additional space or features. If you are not sure which vendor to commit to in the beginning, you can create accounts with several and use them for personal projects for a while to get a sense of the strengths and weaknesses of each one.

Locally Hosted Solutions

If you choose to host your own wiki, you will have many options available to you. Fortunately, many wiki platforms are open source. Open source programs are written by people with the intention that the programs be available for others to use and modify. You should be able to find a wiki platform that is free and part of the open source community. When choosing, it is wise to base your decision on:

- ▶ how commonly the software is used,
- ▶ how active the developer community is, and
- ▶ the strengths the software offers.

When considering an open source option, make sure you investigate the developer community. An active developer community indicates that the platform will continue to improve and that it is likely that you will be able to get software upgrades as needed. An inactive developer community means that you or your technical staff will probably need to create any new customizations or developments you may want.

Finally, you should note that, although open source software has an appealing price tag, you are not really getting the software for free. While you save money in purchasing costs, you will spend more in staff time on the back end. Once you understand all the benefits and drawbacks of open source software and if you are still considering using one, here are a few of the open source options available to you.

If you are specifically interested in documentation of processes or policies, you might want to consider a wiki designed to do exactly that. DokuWiki (www.dokuwiki.org) is an example of a wiki designed specifically for documentation. Figure 2.4 shows a page on the DokuWiki site. Users can easily see older versions and recent changes from buttons at the top of the page, making the site a particularly useful one if you are using it to keep track of library policy or processes.

MediaWiki (www.mediawiki.org) is the most familiar wiki platform (see Figure 2.5), as MediaWiki is the software that powers Wikipedia. MediaWiki's added benefit is that when users edit MediaWiki, they are also learning how to edit Wikipedia, and vice versa. The size of Wikipedia is evidence that MediaWiki is scalable to a size larger than most libraries would require.

If you are particularly interested in getting started with a basic wiki, adding features as you need them, you might be interested in PmWiki (www.pmwiki.org). This wiki platform was designed to be

▶ Figure 2.4: DokuWiki Web Page

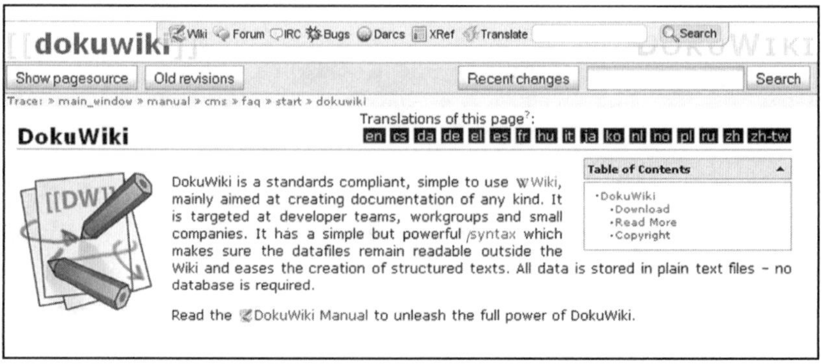

▶ Figure 2.5: MediaWiki Web Page

simple to use with minimal features. However, it's also easy to customize and offers a number of add-ons, making it more useful based on what you choose to add. Figure 2.6 shows the clean design of a PmWiki page that still allows for easy access to all the basic wiki features: editing, reading about its history, and attaching files.

TikiWiki (http://info.tikiwiki.org) is a wiki that considers itself more of a content management system. This platform integrates forums, chat rooms, polls, blogs, file and image galleries, a FAQ, and calendaring into the wiki platform. Notice in Figure 2.7 that the homepages of TikiWiki wikis include a Twitter stream and links

The Wiki Sandbox

Most wikis include a "sandbox." This space is designed for users to experiment with editing a wiki. It is a designated space within a wiki that is safe for people to test out the software, allowing users to make changes without worrying about disrupting the wiki or altering important content. The sandbox can be used to experiment with editing pages, formatting text or layout, or incorporating more advanced features such as widgets or extensions.

▶ Figure 2.6: PmWiki Web Page

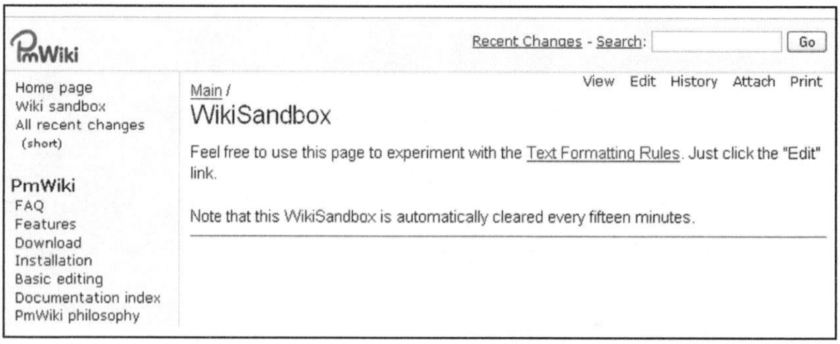

to recent blog posts. TikiWiki is particularly well suited to be the foundation for collaborative and interactive Web sites.

Choosing any of the locally hosted wikis discussed here requires that someone from your library have the capabilities and permissions to install the wiki on your own server space. If you do not have someone on staff who can do this, you could consider hiring a consultant for the initial setup as well as for follow-up support if your wiki needs upgrading or if your library decides that it needs further customization.

Understanding some of the basic features you can expect in a wiki, vendor or locally hosted, gives you enough background to begin thinking about how a wiki might meet your users' needs. Understanding some of the differences between vendor and locally hosted wikis helps you understand what you might need to ask of your technical staff and what your options might be. You will also

► Figure 2.7: TikiWiki Wiki Homepage

want to think about the skill level of your users, the culture of the community, and how you will get buy-in as you plan your wiki.

► ASSESS STAFF AND USER SKILLS

It is now time to consider the human side of wiki implementation. The skills and comfort levels of the staff will have an important impact on their support of and interest in using a wiki. The organizational culture will influence the adoption and use of one. Getting good buy-in from all the staff, whether it was the administration or the front-line workers who initiated the idea, will be important as well. This section will discuss the human side.

Staff Skills

There are a number of skills you will want to consider when thinking about the people who will make the wiki a success. This will help you refine your expectations about the wiki as well as know what it is that you are asking your colleagues to do.

The level of staff skills will impact the costs, in both money and time, associated with creating and maintaining a wiki. If you are planning to host the wiki yourself, and you use an open source option, the expense of the wiki is primarily the cost of the server space and the time the staff spend on creating and maintaining the wiki. Consider both the implementation costs and the recurring maintenance costs of running the wiki. If you do not have a person on staff who knows how to work with open source software, the costs may include consultants to set up the initial site and to do upgrades as they are needed. These costs are minimal if the library already has server space and staff who spend time on projects like this, but it is still worth noting when starting up a project. If you choose, instead, to go with off-site hosting, you might have a solution that is nearly free. Many vendor hosted wikis offer free service in exchange for viewing ads when visiting their site. In addition, wiki setup is often extremely easy, taking no more than 15 minutes. In these cases staff time is negligible, too. Often these free sites have a paid version if you are looking for more space, more features, or fewer advertisements, but this is not often something you need when starting a first wiki.

Another thing to consider is the skill required to create the wiki. As we have discussed, vendor hosted sites do not require specialized skills, but hosting a wiki on your own server does. You will need to either learn these skills yourself or find someone on the staff who has them and is able to help with the project. A larger library, where there is already technical staff, might not have a problem with this. Smaller libraries might be limited in the staff available to help with this type of project and may not even have a position on staff with the skills necessary to create the wiki. In this case, you have to decide if you are able or willing to learn the necessary skills to create the wiki yourself or if you should instead go with a vendor hosted option on the Web.

Once you have created and set up the wiki, time must be available to maintain the wiki. Someone needs to be the primary person responsible for maintaining it. This person does not need to add all the content and read everything everyone writes. He or she should check the wiki for spam and pay attention to the general use of the wiki. If a designated position is accountable for the wiki,

the staff member is more likely to feel responsible for the project and will be in a good position to know when the wiki needs more marketing or when users need more training.

If some library staff members are unfamiliar with wikis, but are expected to participate, you will want to conduct training for them. This training should address both the mechanics of how to edit your specific wiki as well as the organization's expectations for content and participation. Finally, if everyone is expected to participate on some level, you will want to think about how this impacts the staff's ability to do their daily work. If wiki participation is mandated and includes documenting work for the sake of documenting it, this participation just adds to the staff's workload. However, if participation is documenting work so others can perform the work or so the department can continue running when a staff member is out sick or on vacation, participation might actually save staff time in the long run.

Finally, you will want to explore the privacy settings available on your wiki and adjust your wiki in light of the library's expectations. When you are training staff you should clearly state what types of information should be behind the password and what types of information can be public. It is useful to have staff discussions about the purpose of the wiki and the audience when talking about privacy settings.

User Skills

Wiki users are both its readers and its editors. The power of a wiki is in blurring this line between readers and editors. For some library wikis, the wiki user is a library patron. For others, the wiki users are library staff or student employees. No matter who your target audience is, you should think about them when making decisions about your wiki.

One of the first things you will want to think about is the level of computer or technology literacy that you believe your users to have. Will they know that the wiki is a wiki, or will they think that it is a regular Web site? This is important if you expect your audience to contribute to the wiki. If you plan to create a wiki for your audience to use as a Web site, it is less important. If you plan on your audience making edits, you might want to think about their wiki

experience. If you know that you have an audience composed of many people who have edited Wikipedia, you have a strong argument for using MediaWiki. If you know some of your audience has used PBworks for a class or committee, closely consider PBworks.

You will also want to consider the user interface. If the wiki looks fundamentally different from your library's Web site, will your audience be confused? How do you navigate the wiki? Is it easy to find all the information your audience will need? Perhaps you would want to make a page for people who are just getting started that explains how to use the wiki. For librarians, most of whom expect good metadata and organization of information, the search box might not be a preferable way to navigate the wiki. If your primary audience is other library staff, you would want to create a table of contents for the wiki to provide some hierarchy and a map of the information available. You might also want to explore the use of tags or categories to further organize the wiki's information.

Finally, you will also want to think about how to integrate your wiki with library resources. If the wiki is a reference source for your patrons, you will probably want to include links to books and databases on relevant topics. If the wiki provides detailed information about services, you might want to link to specific pages from the library's Web site.

Fitting into an Organizational Culture

In addition to identifying the technical skills that you will want when implementing a wiki, you should also consider the organizational culture. Some institutions have been playing with Web 2.0 technologies for years, and in these libraries it will most likely be easy to pitch a wiki. These communities already have a background where everyone is familiar with the concept of a wiki. There are other libraries that have never considered implementing Web 2.0 technologies for any part of their services. If you are in a library in this position, you might need to educate the library staff as to what a wiki is before suggesting that they use one.

The first cultural point to consider is the staff's experience with Web 2.0 technologies. A staff member who is familiar with Web 2.0 tools and has had positive experiences will likely understand the point of a wiki and in the appropriate situation will support its use.

However, a staff member who has had less positive experiences with a wiki might resist introducing or even using the tool, even if they are already familiar with it. It will probably take a stronger case and implementation plan to convince a staff member in this position that a wiki might be useful.

If you are planning a wiki to support the work that takes place in the library, either as a tool for letting patrons know or as a channel for staff communication, a wise first step is to examine how information is currently being shared within the organization. Is the library fairly transparent in its decision-making and administrative information? If so, a wiki will not challenge the way the library communicates. However, if many decisions are made behind closed doors, or people prefer to keep information quiet within specific levels of the organization, it could be difficult to convince them to move to an open wiki model.

Larger libraries might have to deal with changing communication patterns within the building. If there are silos within the library, where information is not shared easily between teams or departments, it could be a challenge to get everyone on board to participate in the wiki. However, in these settings, it is important to find ways to share information across silos, so there is value in exploring how to implement a wiki as a tool to encourage this type of communication.

Finally, consider the likelihood that staff will contribute. Even if everyone agrees the wiki is a good idea, and fellow staff members are supportive of the wiki's creation, it will not be successful unless you can get a pool of people to contribute. As with any new project, it might be a challenge for your colleagues to find time to contribute. You have to make sure that people feel that contributing to the wiki is valuable if you want them to be successful.

▶ GET STAFF BUY-IN

Luckily, there are many methods you can use to get staff buy-in for a wiki project. If people are behind the project, they will be more likely to contribute, and you will be more likely to have a successful wiki.

The best way to get people on board is to demonstrate a need. You can do this in a number of ways. If patrons are looking for specific information and they are unable to find it, the patrons' needs establish that there is a clear need for a new resource. If the library Webmaster is having difficulty finding enough time to update all the library content in addition to his or her other duties, a wiki will provide a way for staff members to take care of the content while the Webmaster takes care of coding issues. If reference staff find themselves answering the same questions over and over, a wiki site will allow them to create their own information bank where they can collaboratively contribute to answering reference questions. Find a need and show how the wiki will solve it.

Another way of getting people interested in using wikis is to create a pilot project. Using a vendor hosted wiki, you can create a prototype to demonstrate how a wiki would be useful for a specific service or type of information. Once you have worked on the pilot, you will have an idea of the strengths and drawbacks of your approach and can make a good case, supported by evidence, for the use of wikis in a given situation.

Once you know that you will be creating a wiki, you will want to seed the wiki with useful information. People visit wikis only when there is useful information contained in them. To get people interested in and visiting the wiki—even staff for internal wikis—some useful information needs to be there. If you have enough information to get an audience coming, then you have a pool of people who are familiar with the wiki and who can contribute to it. A good source of seeding information is existing documentation. Internal wikis can start with information from staff handouts, meeting minutes, and handbooks. These documents contain information that is relevant to your workplace and have increased value when contained within one searchable Web site.

When starting your wiki, you will want to create training opportunities for the people who you think will want to edit it. These training sessions can address both technical and cultural issues and provide as much support as your users need. In some cases you might want to consider one-on-one training for those who are most unsure about getting started with the wiki.

Finally, a good way of getting people involved with wiki editing is to create a fun wiki for people to practice on. Some groups create "sandbox" wikis, wikis where anything goes. This is a good way for people to feel safe experimenting with all aspects of wiki editing. Because sandbox users know no one will use the sandbox wiki's content in any way, their edits won't misinform anyone. Another technique is to create a non-work-related wiki. This takes some of the pressure off potential users, as those editing the wiki will not hurt anything work related but will still have the opportunity to edit in a real-world setting. If you are interested in this style of a wiki, you could consider creating a staff cookbook, a guide to restaurants in town, or a directory that can include photos, personal statements, and other personal features.

▶3

IMPLEMENTATION

- ▶ **Discover Your Wiki Options**
- ▶ **Start Your Wiki**
- ▶ **Develop Internal Wikis**
- ▶ **Develop External Wikis**
- ▶ **Explore Other Wiki Uses**

Once you have decided to use a wiki, the next step is to think about which type of wiki you would like and how you plan to host it. Think about who will be using the wiki you create and who will set it up. This section of the book includes very basic explanations of how to set up two types of wikis: one that is hosted on a local server and one hosted by a third-party vendor. This background should be enough of a foundation so that you understand the general process of setting up a wiki. Of course, every wiki is slightly different, so if you select a wiki other than one of the two listed here, your process will be slightly different. After explaining how to set up a local or a vendor hosted wiki, the rest of this chapter focuses on different types of implementation you might find useful for your institution.

▶ DISCOVER YOUR WIKI OPTIONS

MediaWiki: A Locally Hosted Option

Many libraries choose to have local installations of a wiki. There are many options for locally hosted wikis. WikiMatrix (www

.wikimatrix.org) may prove most useful to you. The site includes a feature that allows you to specify the requirements you have for your wiki and will respond with a list of wikis that meet those requirements.

For the purposes of an overview, we will discuss MediaWiki. This is the software that runs Wikipedia, which is evidence of its stability, scalability, and community of support. Because this is the software that runs Wikipedia, you might find that a number of your potential wiki editors are already familiar with how to edit your wiki.

Manual Installation

The first decision you will make when installing a wiki is where you will install it. If you have a person on your staff in charge of the Web site, this might be a good person to approach. If you will be tackling the project, you will want to look at the software's Web site and see if there is a page for system administrators or installation. For example, when using MediaWiki, you will begin with the page shown in Figure 3.1.

► Figure 3.1: MediaWiki's Download Page

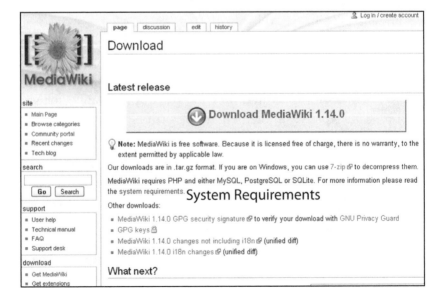

The page in Figure 3.1 shows both the link to download the MediaWiki software and a link to MediaWiki's specific system requirements. MediaWiki requires access to a specific type of Web server that would allow you to install the software. The page explains that the Web server needs to support the use of PHP, a programming language primarily for the Web that MediaWiki uses. This Web server will also need to be able to communicate with a MySQL database, which is where the wiki content will be stored. Your technology staff will know if you have these capabilities. Discuss the list of system requirements with your technology staff or service provider to get an accurate understanding of whether you have the system to support the wiki.

Once you know where you will put the wiki, the next step in creating a MediaWiki site is to create a database. In the case of MediaWiki, you would need to create a MySQL database and a user. Once you have set up this foundation, you can download the software you plan to use and upload it to your account using FTP. You create a folder to extract these files to, and, once extracted, this will be the wiki location. MediaWiki will then prompt you to set up your wiki. To do so, you will follow a link to the installation page, and configure your wiki, including the name for your site, contact e-mail, language, and license. You will be asked to configure your database as well. Once you have been through all of the steps, you will be presented with an "Install" link, and clicking that link will complete the process.

Automated Installation

Depending on your system, you might have the option for a simpler installation of your wiki. Some Web hosting services, such as DreamHost (www.dreamhost.com), offer a "one click install" that allows users to click a button to automatically install MediaWiki, as well as other Web applications. This method is nearly as simple as it sounds. You click an install button, and the software walks you through the installation process. You will need to answer a few questions as you go through the process regarding specific wiki settings.

Configuration

Once you have MediaWiki on your server, you can configure it to fit your needs. Following the directions on the Web site, you point your browser to a specific URL, and then you are given a list of configuration options. This is the point where you choose privacy options, the wiki styles, and other basic setup details. On one hand, it is useful that MediaWiki guides you through the process, but it is also worth noting that, if you run into trouble, there is much more information on the MediaWiki Web site (see Figure 3.2). Again, if you choose a wiki with an active developer community, you will likely find a similar resource for any installed options.

If you selected a locally hosted wiki so that you could have more control over its aesthetic design or privacy settings, this is when you would begin work in those areas. If you are technically inclined and comfortable experimenting with the site, this may be a simple process. If you are less technically inclined, you may want to contact your technical staff to see if this is something they can do for you. You might also want to consider a vendor hosted option to avoid these steps altogether.

▶ Figure 3.2: MediaWiki Help Page

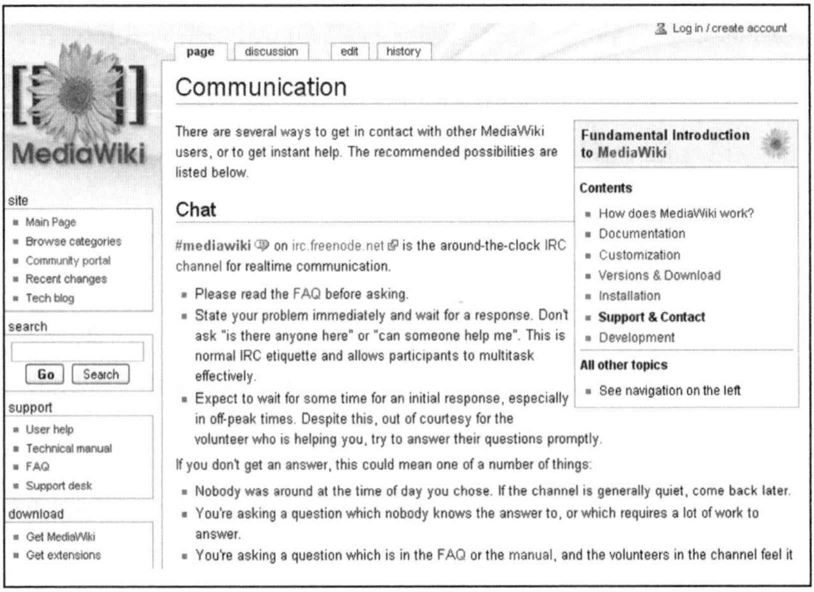

Customization

You can customize a number of things within your wiki. You might want to change the look of the wiki or some part of the layout. You can do some basic customization within the wiki, and you can make other changes by modifying the wiki's theme or style sheet. The style sheet allows the Webmaster to make changes to one file that impact the look of every page on the wiki.

You can also make personal customizations. This is where you modify the look of the wiki that you see when you log in to the wiki. If you just want to make a basic change, you can click on "My Preferences" once you have installed and logged into the wiki. From there you can change the theme settings.

Preparing to Go Live

Before releasing your wiki to the staff or to the public, you will want to do some work behind the scenes. The rest of this chapter will address specifics for setting up different versions of a wiki for your library. But regardless, you will want to set up the basic framework and seed the wiki with some basic information to get people started. You will want to set up privacy and permissions appropriate to the use of the wiki. For example, perhaps you want everyone in the world to be able to see a page for the community book club. You might want everyone to see the library mission page but only the director to edit it. You might want the library staff meeting minutes to be available only to staff. You can set up these permissions in most wikis as you create the site.

PBworks: A Vendor Hosted Option

If you need a wiki quickly, are planning to use it for a small project, and you are not planning on putting any sensitive data on it, you have some good reasons to select a vendor hosted option. These hosted options can help people become familiar with wikis without too much technical overhead. Many people who start with a vendor hosted wiki end up hosting their own later on. If you suspect this might be the case for you, consider how you will move the data from the vendor hosted wiki to the local one if that time comes. There are many options for vendor hosted wikis just as there are for locally hosted ones. Again, you can find a list of wikis with a simple Google search, or use a site like WikiMatrix to find one that meets your requirements.

For the purposes of this overview, we will discuss PBworks. This provider has become very popular with libraries and has an emphasis on supporting educational uses. PBworks has recently redefined itself to focus on easy collaboration, so you might find it more functional than some of the other providers available on the Web.

PBworks, as with many vendor hosted options, has several account levels. There is a basic free account, but there are also paid accounts with more features and options. It is always a good idea to pilot a free account to make sure the wiki meets your needs before committing to a larger, more costly account. You will often get better customer support and more customizations with paid accounts.

Creating an Account

When starting your PBworks wiki, you will need to create an account with some basic information. Once you have submitted this, you will be able to create your wiki. PBworks prides itself on the ease of setting up its wikis, and it should be a fairly quick and familiar process for anyone who has registered with a social Web site in the past. Notice in Figure 3.3 that PBworks simply asks for the URL, why you are using it, and what type of organization and workplace purpose you have for creating the site.

Editing a Vendor Hosted Wiki

When you log into PBworks for the first time, you will see a page with basic information about your wiki. When you click on the "Edit" tab you will see the screen shown in Figure 3.4. This page displays the content as well as a bar of buttons similar to what you would see in Word or Google Docs.

PBworks uses a "What You See Is What You Get" (WYSIWYG) editor. This means that you do not have to know any code to format the text the way you want it to look. Just click on the buttons to make bold text, links, or bulleted lists. Once you have made the changes you want to keep, click "Save," and the page is created, just like that.

▶ Figure 3.3: PBworks Sign-Up Page

▶ Figure 3.4: PBworks Editing Page

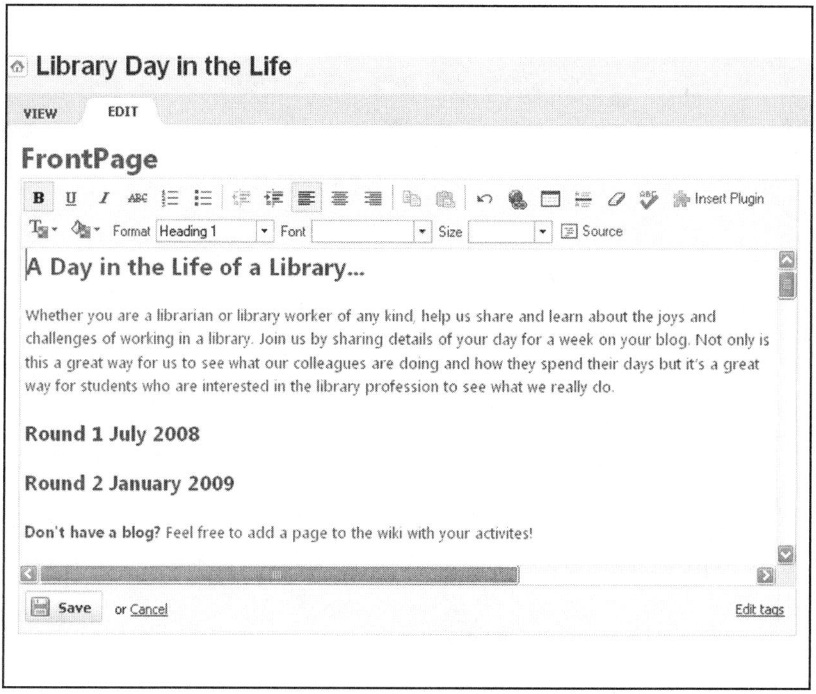

Personalizing a Vendor Hosted Wiki

There are a number of things that you can customize within your hosted wiki. You might want to change the colors of the wiki or some of the privacy settings. How much customization, and how to make these changes, varies from wiki to wiki. In PBworks, you will want to explore the "Settings" tab. This tab has options for changing the colors, logos, user access, and more advanced alterations. Figure 3.5 shows PBworks' "Settings" tab. On the settings page you can adjust the colors of your site and add your organization's logo to the wiki. You can also use Access Controls to add specific users to the wiki, adjust security, and set up notifications for when the wiki is modified.

▶ START YOUR WIKI

Just as in the MediaWiki example, before releasing your wiki to the staff or the public you will want to do some work behind the scenes. Providing a basic framework and basic information and set-

▶ Figure 3.5: PBworks Settings Page

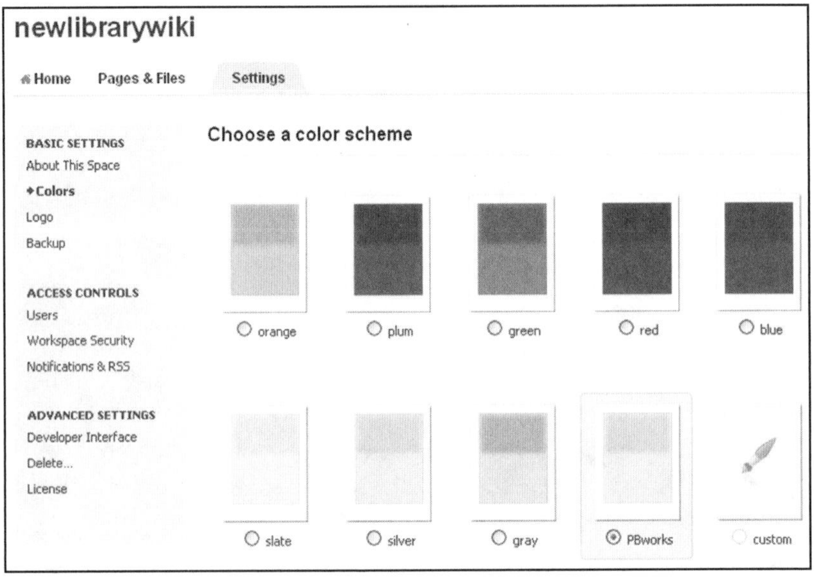

ting appropriate privacy controls and permissions will help your audience understand the way to use the wiki for your project and how they can participate.

Extending Your Wiki

In the past several years, there has been a large growth in a type of Internet tool referred to as a "widget." Widgets are small parts of Web sites that you can include on other Web sites with minimal technology skills. For example, if you keep a Google Calendar, you can use a Google Calendar widget to pull a small version of the calendar into your wiki. If you use chat reference, there are widgets to embed a chat box on another Web page. If you use Twitter, you can pull that over, too. Widgets are a way to give your wiki additional functionality while also making the site more engaging for the user. An added benefit is that anytime you update information on these other sites, the information is automatically updated in your wiki. You do not have to remember to update things in more than one place.

If you are hosting your own wiki, you will want to consider extensions, features beyond the ones that come with the basic wiki software, that you can add to your wiki. Look for extensions, add-ons, or plug-ins that allow your wiki to do more, such as change the way the text displays on a page, the way you can edit content, the type of media that you can include, or statistics you are able to keep. This work would likely be done by the person who was involved with the technical side of installing the wiki. So, if you are hiring a consultant to install your wiki, you will want to think about extensions while the consultant is working on your project.

PBworks and other vendor hosted wikis often integrate widgets into their wikis. Look for links to "Insert Plug-In" or "Add Multimedia" to add this type of functionality to your vendor hosted wiki. It is worth noting that not all wikis will offer all the same plug-ins, so if you are thinking about this and have decided that you know of something that you will need to add, this might be a factor to use in selecting your wiki provider.

Wiki Extensions

The available options for extending your wiki will vary depending on the software that runs the site. If you are using MediaWiki, you will have a number of options:

- ▶ **GISWiki kwBreadCrumbs**: This "bread crumbs" extension (www.mediawiki.org/wiki/Extension:GISWiki_kwBread Crumbs) enables links to appear at the top of the wiki page, showing users their path to their present location within the wiki, and allowing them to click back to the page they are most interested in.
- ▶ **Bibwiki**: This useful extension (www.mediawiki.org/wiki/ Extension:Bibwiki) was written to make it easier to create and manage scientific bibliographies and is especially helpful in libraries.
- ▶ **YouTube Tag**: You might be interested in incorporating multimedia into your wiki. This extension (www.mediawiki.org/wiki/Extension:YouTubeTag) allows you to pull in a video from YouTube.
- ▶ **FireStats**: If you are interested in collecting statistics for the use of your wiki, you might want to consider this extension (www.mediawiki.org/wiki/Extension:FireStats) to help collect that data.

Once you are comfortable with MediaWiki, and have an idea of something you would like to be able to do within your site, you should search the Internet to see if someone has created the extension that will meet your needs. MediaWiki has a large and active developer community, and due to this you can find many interesting extensions. You can find more information about MediaWiki extensions at www.mediawiki.org/wiki/Category:Extensions.

PBworks also offers this type of increased functionality; however, the PBworks community refers to them as plug-ins. These plug-ins are built into every PBworks wiki. PBworks organizes their plug-ins by categories, such as office applications, HTML, gadgets, page information, video, photos, and interactive media. Some of these plug-ins pull in content from other sites, such as Google or YouTube. Others make use of services like Skype. Yet, you still have tremendous flexibility with the HTML plug-in option, as long as you are comfortable with HTML.

Early Wiki Questions

While you are early in the process of creating your wiki, you will need to consider several issues. Thinking about these topics early in your implementation will guide you through the process and help you have a more successful wiki.

1. What is the mission statement of your wiki? How does it relate to the mission of your library?
2. Who should be able to read the wiki content?
3. Who should have the ability to edit the wiki content?
4. Where will you host the wiki?
5. Who will add seed content? Where will they get this content?
6. How will you market your wiki?

▶ DEVELOP INTERNAL WIKIS

How to Create a Wiki Intranet

A wiki can be useful as an intranet for your library. It is easy to set up, and all that the library employees need to know is the URL to access it. Employees can get to the information online from the library, away at conferences, and at home. Figure 3.6 shows an ex-

▶ Figure 3.6: Wiki as an Intranet

ample of the University of Minnesota Libraries' wiki intranet. As you can see, the wiki contains vision and mission statements as well as announcements and links to library staff sites. The site also contains other relevant information, including the library organizational chart and information on budgets and planning.

An intranet is a portal for internal use by an organization. This portal can contain reference information about the business, files such as images or documents that employees might need to use on a regular basis, and information about upcoming events and scheduling, as the University of Minnesota wiki does. For example, you might find the following in an intranet site:

▶ Announcements

▶ The library's schedule of events

▶ Reminders about upcoming deadlines

▶ Current room availability

▶ Meeting minutes

▶ Forms such as timesheets and vacation requests

Intranets are often protected with passwords so that information can be included that would typically go in a handbook behind a desk.

Knowing that you can embed other content and use widgets to extend your wiki, you may choose a wiki designed to simplify the process of adding calendar entries, embedding useful widgets, or adding other multimedia content. Think about the gadgets that will make the wiki more valuable and engaging and where you will put them in the wiki. When thinking about widgets, it is worth considering which ones will streamline your input process rather than duplicate it. If you are already updating a 30 box calendar, look for a widget to import that content into the wiki automatically rather than creating a second calendar within the wiki.

When starting an intranet, you will want to think about how to set it up before you start putting work into adding content. What information will people expect to find? What information is important enough to include on the front page? Should you use a hierarchical organization or something more flexible such as tagging or search? It is worth talking to other staff members about their expectations and interests so that you can best design the intranet to fit their needs. You will also want to talk to colleagues to get a broad sense of the overall information issues of the organization. Once you have some basic ideas, it would be a good idea to begin developing a FAQ page to let people know what to contribute and how. Taking a little time to do this in the beginning will save you a lot of time in answering e-mails and fielding questions in the long run.

Once you have figured out the basic information that people will be interested in knowing, you will need to get the content. In some cases, you will be able to start up sections by yourself. Other topics will require content from others who have subject expertise. For example, if you work in archives, you might want to talk with someone from reference to see if he or she can write up some information to start off the reference section of the wiki. If you want to make it really easy to contribute, you could just ask for the content in Word format and enter it into the wiki yourself. Incorporating this basic information at an early stage ensures that the other library staff members will find the wiki useful enough to return and hopefully to contribute themselves.

Once you have set up the basic wiki outline, you will want to make sure that someone from each department will keep an eye on the wiki for content related to their department. To make the wiki a valuable intranet, information will need to be current and accurate. Designating a person from each unit means that someone is responsible and will be more likely to check in every once in a while. This could be a permanent function for some positions, or it could be a committee with rotating membership.

Once you have a wiki, a basic outline, seeded content, and designated wiki editors, all that is left to do is to roll the wiki out to the rest of the staff. This approach will vary depending on the culture of your library. If people are fairly comfortable with new technologies, you may choose to mention the wiki in a staff meeting, send the link out, and offer to be available if there are questions. If people are very hesitant about new tools, you might need to offer a series of staff development sessions, teaching people about how wikis work, how to edit them, and how to use your wiki to find and share information. In any case, your coworkers will appreciate having someone they can call if they have a question. You might be the point person, but the designated editors in each department will also be good resources for the rest of the staff. It is best if you can get a broad group to participate in this work so that people do not think of it as your wiki. You really do want the wiki to be a community project!

Incorporating the wiki into the workflow of your place of employment will largely depend on the vision of your library administration. If they see the wiki as a supplemental tool, you might continue using traditional patterns of communication within the library but also include links to the pages in the wiki that have the same content. If they see the wiki as a way to decrease e-mail, meeting time, and communication gaps, they might have a stronger investment in supporting the use of a wiki. If the administration is solidly behind the wiki, you will need to help people remember to use the wiki and where to look for information.

How to Create a Wiki Knowledge Base

Wikis also make strong knowledge bases. Knowledge bases are resources that provide access to information. They commonly exist at help desks or to share information about the different work within the organization. A knowledge base could be helpful at the reference desk for questions that are very specific but common enough to be predictable, at the circulation desk to keep staff abreast of the most recent policies, or even for student workers, a group with a very high turnover yet who still need a lot of needed knowledge for their work.

Knowledge bases often make great first wikis for an organization. You can pick a specific department and create a small wiki for its use. As it becomes more successful, and people get used to it, the idea will spread throughout the organization. You can get a sense of what works for your organization and how people use it, which, in turn, can inform your future wiki work.

When setting up a knowledge base, you will need to decide if it will be a searchable FAQ or if you are going to have a hierarchical reference source. This, of course, depends on the context your wiki will be used in. If you are creating a resource for student employees, you might design the wiki content to read like a handbook so that they can read it in their first week on the job. The wiki will still need to function as a knowledge base, though, so students will need to be able to search the wiki as well in order to get to information at the point in time when they need it. This is a great system because so many students work when full-time staff members are not in the building. This is a resource they can consult in the early hours of the morning—getting the information a patron needs at that moment—instead of leaving a note for a staff member to deal with first thing in the morning. If, instead, the wiki will be primarily for full-time staff who are already acclimated to the environment, you might not need as much narrative structure. A simple list of questions could suffice.

To start a knowledge base wiki, you can include a list of common departmental questions. Then, you can brainstorm additional questions with your department. Besides generating more questions, brainstorming will help participants buy into the project as they are being included in the creation of the resource.

Whereas with the intranet you would want to seed the wiki with enough information to be useful enough to draw staff members in, this might not be necessary for a knowledge base wiki. If staff have really bought into the concept of a knowledge base and can see how it could save them time or help patrons get better service even when the staff are not around, you may be able to start with just a list of questions. Or, you might even be able to start with a few open-ended questions about whether people can figure out how to fit the new knowledge base into their workflow.

If the knowledge base wiki is not accepted by its audience, you can begin targeting a smaller audience focusing on those who would benefit the most from it. For example, a busy reference desk with a lot of complex business questions could benefit from having the answers to complex business questions and steps for finding the relevant information. This will help everyone at the desk find the answers quickly and will help the business librarian regain some uninterrupted time in the office.

When deciding how to set up the wiki, you will also need to consider how to convey the information most effectively. For example, if the questions are about a physical task—labeling books, loading microfilm, or fixing paper jams—you may consider including embedded videos demonstrating how to accomplish these tasks. However, if these videos are likely to be watched at a public desk, you would want to make silent videos, with text overlaid on the images, so as not to disturb patrons.

Again, you will want to think about colleagues who could support the wiki as well. Getting a few people on board will make the whole process easier and will mean that you are not doing all of the work yourself. It also will make the project be more of a grassroots effort and more likely to spread through the entire staff.

Once you have some content in your knowledge base and you have trained people to use the site or offered to help, you are ready to put the wiki in production. Posting the link near departmental computers, making the wiki the homepage for the browser, or stopping by people's offices to show them the wiki and walk them through using it are all methods of helping colleagues get on board with the new wiki.

If the wiki acts as a handbook, you can ask the people who have read the content what is still unclear and incorporate that content into the wiki for the next user. The whole point of using the wiki is that it is easy to update content in this way. If the site is a FAQ wiki, you can point out to desk workers that they can check it as they get questions. If the answer is there, the wiki will be helpful; if the answer is not, they can contribute it.

Figure 3.7 shows the Wake Forest (NC) University Z. Smith Reynolds Library knowledge base wiki. This wiki is organized by department and includes a few library-wide project categories as well. Each department page contains links to other pages within the wiki that explain processes or make meeting minutes available.

How to Use Wikis for Facilitated Collaboration within a Library

Wikis also help facilitate collaboration within a library. Small committees, task forces, and groups working on a common project can use a wiki to facilitate this work. The wiki can be a home base for the work of the group. It can include the objectives and specifications of the project, meeting minutes, discussions about the group's tasks, and even allow space for drafting out written work.

▶ Figure 3.7: Wiki as a Knowledge Base

Sometimes you can look for things that are fun to communicate about to get people interested in using a wiki. My library, for example, shares recipes after potluck lunches or other special occasions. These recipes were listed in a "cookbook" on the library's Web site. But to get the recipe listed, an individual had to rely on the Webmaster to add the content to the site. One of the first sections of the library wiki was our cookbook. The idea was to take something we already enjoyed doing and use the wiki to facilitate that behavior.

Once people are comfortable with using a wiki collaboratively, you can use the wiki to facilitate work within the library. Durham County (NC) Library used a wiki for their strategic planning process, as shown in Figure 3.8. This wiki includes goals, documents

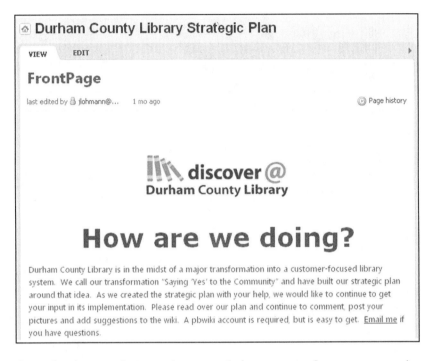

▶ Figure 3.8: Wiki for Internal Collaboration

from brainstorming sessions, and comments from community members on the future of the library.

When working with a small group to set up a wiki to facilitate collaboration, you have the luxury of coming to consensus. You will want to discuss what channels you will be using and how much information goes on the wiki. Will you avoid e-mail altogether and rely on everyone to check into the wiki once a day? Maybe you will put all the information in the wiki and send a message to the group reminding them to check in when you update it? Or, maybe you will e-mail and meet as always but add the information to the wiki, too, so it is all in one place.

Once everyone is in agreement, you should be able to create a framework that fits with the expectations of the group members. With a small group, you can rely on the different members to contribute as is relevant to their position within the group. You might want to designate a note-taker to ensure meeting minutes are all in one place. Perhaps committee homework assignments include updating different sections with content.

You might want to think about vendor and locally hosted options specifically designed for internal work. If any information is sensitive, you will probably prefer to investigate local options. If information is not sensitive, and you want to trade files, you might choose to go with a third-party vendor that makes it easy to share files through the wiki.

How to Use Wikis for Facilitated Collaboration with People at Other Locations

Wikis can facilitate collaboration whether participants are geographically nearby or across the country. Many professional committees use wikis to collaborate across long distances. Particularly if a committee is national in scope, and members see each other only twice a year, it is helpful to have a virtual workspace in the interim. A wiki can be an ideal solution in a situation like this.

When setting up a wiki for this type of work, you will want to identify the types of wikis that everyone is comfortable using. If people already edit Wikipedia, for example, it is worth asking if any of the committee members can host a MediaWiki option on their server. Or, if everyone already has a PBworks log in, the group might choose to host their wiki there to streamline their wiki work. It is likely that everyone will have a different background; in this case the group might need to discuss what options everyone is comfortable with using.

In the course of that discussion, you will also want to address how you will be using the wiki. Is it mostly for conversation? Brainstorming? Holding final drafts of committee work for review? These decisions will likely influence what wiki you choose and how you set it up. BIGWIG, an interest group of the Library Information Technology Association (LITA), uses wiki space within the larger LITA wiki, as shown in Figure 3.9. In this case, you can see that the wiki contains meeting minutes, information about three upcoming projects, and a link to information for their conference. Each project includes some basic background, a space for people to sign up to volunteer, as well as next steps for the group to accomplish. This is a collaborative space that also produces final products for others to view. These documents are sometimes hosted on

► Figure 3.9: Wiki for Collaboration with Other Libraries

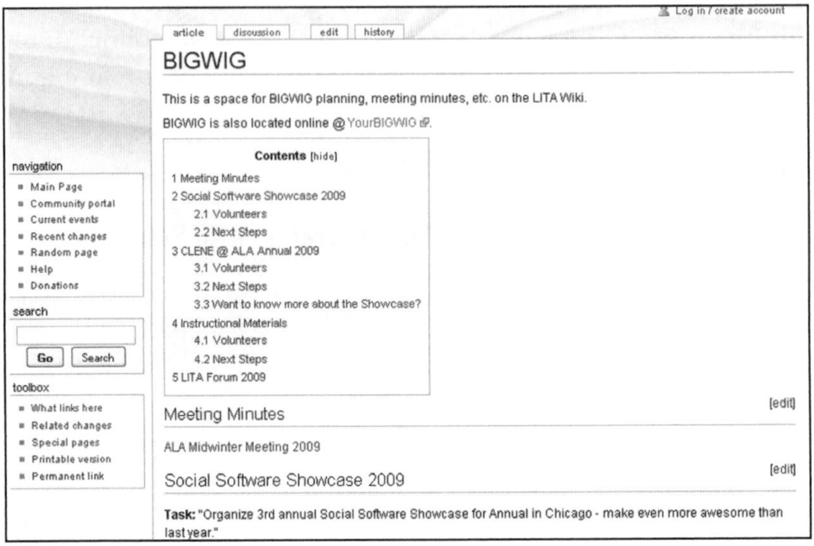

the wiki for others to see and other times are migrated to other publication platforms.

If you set up a wiki to use with people in other locations, you will want to think about the site's organization and discuss your plans with the other committee members. You might choose to designate one area for notes, one for discussion, one for brainstorming and preliminary work, and one for work that is approaching the final version of the committee's product. If the committee belongs to a larger organization, you might also want to include some information for visitors who are not part of your wiki. Again, a relevant wiki takes some planning and scaffolding. You will want to include some places where people can add content as it comes up, and you will want to work with others to make sure they feel comfortable contributing.

How to Use Wikis for Project Management

Wikis can also be useful tools for project management. When working on a project, you will need to record many pieces of information: the desired outcomes, requirements to meet the goals, deadlines, meeting minutes, tasks to be done, and responsible individuals. Keeping all of this information in one central place allows project team members to know where to find authoritative information and how to record the work that they have done. This has the added benefit of making it easy to share progress with supervisors and other stakeholders so that everyone is clear on what the project's aims are and if the project is meeting its timeline.

Figure 3.10 shows the Lupton Library's Building Project from the University of Tennessee–Chattanooga. This wiki contains the official announcement, the program statement, and suggested visit information for those involved. The wiki brings transparency to the Library Building Project and allows interested people to follow along with the progress of the group.

One way to help a new project succeed is to build in early wins. You can do this when you are planning how you will use the wiki as a project management tool. In the very first meeting, for example, you can have the wiki open and projecting on a screen. You can take minutes directly in the wiki, add dates and deadlines, and then e-mail links out to committee members while they are all present. Everyone will see that the wiki saves time because you won't need to go back to your desk to type up formal notes, send e-mails back and forth, and negotiate out information through other channels. Members will also see the information going into

▶ Figure 3.10: Wiki for Project Management

the wiki and know that they can turn to it for answers to those questions. Hopefully, in seeing how easy it is to edit, they will also know that they can go in and make updates as they accomplish tasks. In this case there would be two wins: demonstrating an immediate and obvious connection between saving time and using the wiki and providing an informal example of how easy it is to edit a wiki.

When in that first meeting, you will want to discuss the types of information you would like to include and how authoritative the resource will need to be. You will want to organize the information in a way that will be easy for participating committee members to understand, but if you are planning to share the content with other stakeholders, you will want to organize the wiki so that it will be intuitive to navigate for their purposes as well. You might include a link on the front page for committee members and a link for stakeholders. Then, you can have an index designed for each group individually. For example, you would probably choose to include a link in both indexes to the timeline but a link to discussion for committee members only. Some wikis will also let you share pages with different configurations of people, so you might make use of this feature as well.

You will again want to designate who is responsible for what. The person ultimately responsible for the project may choose to monitor the use of the wiki. In checking in regularly, the wiki monitor will see what has not happened and what the group's next actions should be. This will help the monitor follow up with individuals as they work, too.

If there is buy-in early in the process, you will not need to push too much to market the wiki. However, if there is not an early win, you will want to help people get comfortable with using the wiki as the group progresses through its goals. You might do this by meeting one-on-one with each participant to walk him or her through the process or, if people want to add information, volunteer to do it with them.

If everyone understands that the project wiki is the source of information about the project's status, it should be easy to incorporate it into workflow. This also means that once the project is complete, there will be documentation for people if others have to repeat the project later or if someone needs to modify some aspect of the work after someone has left the organization.

These internal uses of wikis are designed to make work easier and communication simpler. Internal wikis also allow members of the organization to access information at the point in time when they need it.

▶ DEVELOP EXTERNAL WIKIS

So far we have focused on ways to use a wiki internally. Internal wikis are often good places to start. The staff is generally a smaller audience than the library's community would be, so your risk is smaller. You tend to know the people you work with, so you can ask for opinions more easily than you can with the entire library community. If the wiki doesn't work with the staff, you can step back, reevaluate, and try another one with a different implementation. This can be harder to do with a larger, more general audience. Starting internally will help you understand how your colleagues feel about using a wiki, how they will incorporate it into their workflow, and how it will impact how the library works.

Once you suspect a wiki will be useful for your library, you might start to consider how a wiki could be a solution for external communication and collaboration as well. Or, perhaps you have the perfect situation for using a wiki, and now you will be working on your colleagues to help them understand how a wiki will help the community. You might consider using a wiki to create a Web site for the library, to create a site for a special event, to be a collaborative resource or a subject guide, or to be part of your instructional toolkit. This section will address these external uses of wikis.

How to Create a Wiki Web Site

Some organizations use wikis to run their Web site. This is true for organizations of all different types and sizes, and it can be true for libraries, too.

For example, Figure 3.11 shows the University of South Carolina Aiken Gregg Graniteville Library Web site. This Web site was built using a wiki, but it still retains features common to library

▶ Figure 3.11: Wiki Web Site

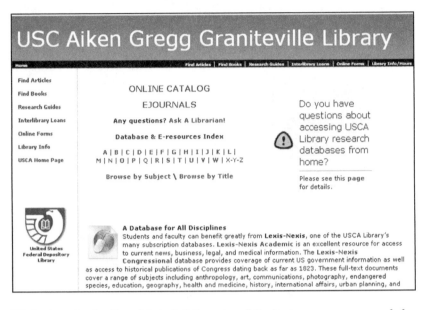

Web sites, including "Ask A Librarian," links to resources, and database information.

If you choose to use a wiki to host your library Web site, you may want to look into ways to make the site look less like a wiki. If you have a Webmaster on staff who is familiar with CSS (cascading style sheets), he or she can adjust the style to look less like a wiki. The Webmaster can remove the "Edit" tabs from pages, and give the site the colors and logos that are familiar to your users. If you are hosting it yourself, you can locate the site at your current URL so that patrons can continue using their own bookmarks. If you were to use a vendor hosted option, you would probably need to look into redirecting the URL to your current library address so that a strange domain doesn't confuse your users. A vendor hosted site will give you less control of the look of your wiki, but again this depends on the provider you are using and the level of membership you have.

When setting up a wiki Web site, you will want to take the same approaches that you would take when creating your own Web site. Initially, you might want to make the wiki Web site look and act as much like your regular Web site as possible so that your users will not be too confused by the new site and its organization. Of course, some libraries redesign their Web sites from scratch and release the new version with an education campaign, so you might choose this path and redesign your Web site from scratch with the new wiki site. If you do redesign your Web site you might want to hold focus groups with various constituencies—library board, users, students, faculty, parents, staff members—to see what expectations people have of the Web site, what they really like and would not want to lose, and what is missing from the current design. You can use this information to create a Web site that better fits the needs of your users based on what they actually request.

When doing this, you will already have most of the information you will want to include—it is already on your Web site! To save time, you can copy this information into the new Web site. Assuming your current Web site is up-to-date, you will know the information is accurate and timely.

Now, the people who were responsible for contributing to the Web site are probably likely candidates for contributing to this new Web site. However, if the contributors had been limited to folks who understood HTML, you now can consider a broader pool of candidates. The Web site could even be opened up to everyone, if administration felt comfortable with that.

Because the Web site is typically an important source of information about your library, and with the wiki structure anyone can save changes, you might consider how to get the appropriate signoff on changes to the Web site. You might have people add suggested changes to the discussion section of a page, or even submit it to a specific page of the wiki designated for changes. Then, once a week or once a month, appropriately ranked staff members could make the changes or let people know that changes have been approved and can be made.

You will probably also want to establish a workflow for this new initiative. This workflow gives you a process that you can train people to follow and makes it clear to everyone how changes will work and who can make them. If everyone can learn the process and how to make the changes, it will inevitably save you and the technology-savvy staff members the time and burden of making all of the changes to the wiki.

You might, at this point, worry about what happens if someone makes a malicious change without approval. This tends to happen far less frequently than we worry about in work and classroom settings. People know they will be held accountable if they make a change and will not risk damage to their position or their grade. However, you might have someone who has nothing to lose make a change. Because most wikis make reverting to a previous version of any given page very easy, you can quickly get back the content as it was before it was damaged.

Library patrons do not need to know that the library Web site is a wiki, although they might need to be notified that they have a new library Web site. You will probably want to do standard user education to let them know what to expect out of the site and its organization. Library staff members who do not edit the wiki will need the same training. Those staff who will be editing will need an introduction to the new site, instructions on how to edit and where to put information, and training on what expectations are for editing the site.

How to Create a Special Event Wiki

A wiki can be a good solution if you are creating a Web site for a special event but do not want to bother your Webmaster with the regular updates you are planning to make. A wiki may require only an initial setup, which may impact your technology staff if it is locally hosted and would impact event organizers only if it is hosted by a third-party provider.

If you choose to host the wiki yourself, you will need to work with a Webmaster when setting up the wiki. This initial work will ensure that the site is up and running and has the basic theme that you want it to have. If you have the logo and color scheme at this early stage, you can work with the Webmaster to ensure that the site has an appropriate appearance. Once the Webmaster has set up the back end, or you have set up a third-party site to meet your requirements, you are ready to start adding content.

LITA used a third-party site to host a wiki for their recent camp. Notice, in Figure 3.12, that the page was not open for editing by participants. This wiki included content relevant to the event, including sponsors, a link to related social software, registration, the

▶ Figure 3.12: Special Events Wiki

schedule, and a FAQ. After the camp was completed the site included information about what happened at the event. The wiki
transitioned from an active site promoting the event before it happened to one archiving and preserving the event once it was over.

Like any upcoming event site, you will want to design your wiki
to include relevant information for the participants you are targeting. If you are planning a lecture series, you will want to include
when, where, and who will be speaking. Your audience will find it
useful to include an image of the speaker and a biography. You
may consider embedding video footage of the speaker at another
event. If you are planning a workshop or conference, you might
start the wiki with just an announcement. As you figure out more
about what is going to happen at the conference, what hotel will
offer a discount, who the keynote speaker will be, and all the other
conference details, you will want to add this information to the
Web site.

If you are starting the wiki site early on, before many decisions
are made, you might not need to organize much information. A
site early in the planning cycle could consist of just a front page

with a list of all the current information. However, as you get closer and closer to the event, you will have more to share. Think about having a section on the front page for news, and as you develop other wiki content you can create entire wiki pages devoted to it.

If the library is small and only one person is organizing the event, that person would also be in charge of the wiki. Many libraries planning events might have a staff member or committee focused on marketing. In this case, the marketer may be in charge of the wiki. Large events, with subcommittees focused on different aspects of the project, might benefit from assigning a person on each subcommittee with updating their group's portion of the wiki.

If you are using a wiki to market an event, it makes sense to use the wiki to hold the planning documents as well. This will keep all your project information in one place. However, it is understandable that you may not want your event participants to have access to the documents you were using to plan the event. In this case, you can make these pages private for the event staff. They will be hidden from the participants but still be available for the people who will need them.

You will want to market the wiki to your users the same way that you would market any event Web site to the public. You might create flyers with the URL, make bookmarks that are distributed at circulation, or add a line about it to e-mail signatures from the reference desk. Essentially, though, a special events wiki is a marketing piece for an event, so you will just want to include the URL anywhere you are mentioning the event—your Web site, newspaper and radio advertisements, evening news stories—anywhere people will learn about the event. If your event is targeting a broad audience, for example, a statewide book or something new to your community, you might consider buying Google AdWords as part of your marketing strategy. This will help people searching for similar information find your wiki, even if they are not your library's typical audience.

How to Create a Wiki Online Resource

As you probably understand by now, wikis are highly flexible. You can use them to meet a variety of needs and interests. Some libraries might want to create their own resource. For example, in Figure 3.13 you can see a wiki that the Guilford County, North Carolina, librarians created to provide information about their community for their community. This wiki contains information about the site for potential users, explaining the Librarian's Guide to Guilford County. It contains basic information about the community on the front page, and links in the sidebar point to areas of specific interest, such as "Books and Reading," "Education," and "Events."

Similarly, you might want to create a local history Web site or a site about your special collections. Maybe you want to create a Web site for people interested in your larger organization, school, or university. A wiki can make it easy to do so.

Presumably, you are coming to the project with a specific information need in your community. You have likely gained an understanding of community needs and interests from your work in the library. This background will help you know if a resource is needed and if the library has people in a position to create one.

You will want to decide who will be involved in this project and what their roles will be. Will participants want to find information and give it to you to enter in the wiki? Will they be comfortable

▶ Figure 3.13: Online Resource Wiki

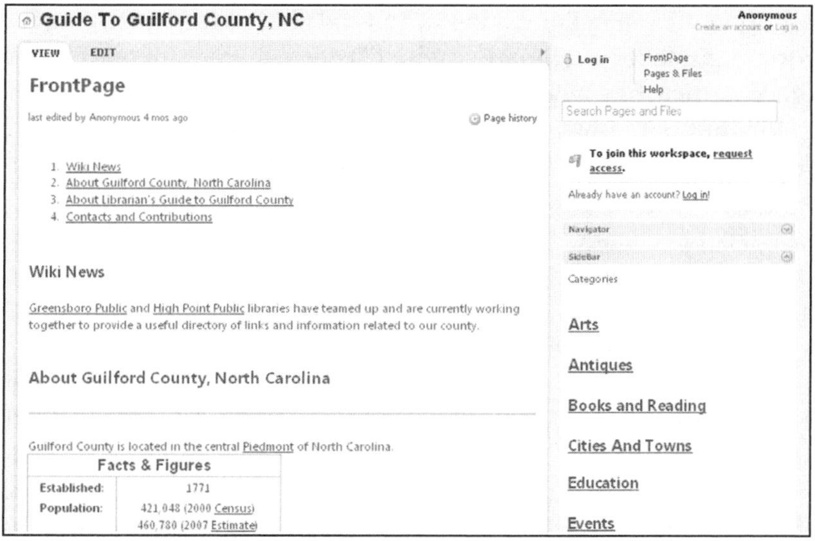

with all stages of the project and be able to handle everything from finding the information to editing the information to entering content into the site?

If you are getting others involved before making the site public, you can use the wiki much as you would an internal project wiki as you are working. Then, before releasing the wiki, participants will want to clean up the wiki content and remove or password protect pages that are not relevant to users interested in the topic. This will streamline the workflow process for you and your colleagues and remove any information your users would find confusing.

When marketing an online resource wiki, you will want to use the techniques that you have developed for marketing other online resources: digital collections, electronic databases, or virtual reference. You will want to market it within your library building, in local media outlets, as well as to people interested in the specific issue your site is dealing with. You can do this by e-mailing groups, writing up articles for relevant publications, or, again, by buying Google AdWords. The main goal is to get the wiki in the public where people can find it.

How to Create a Wiki Subject Guide

Libraries often have a number of subject guides. These handouts and Web sites help users find authoritative and relevant content on a specific topic. For example, an academic library might have a subject guide for freshman English classes to help students find literary criticism articles, relevant reference resources, citation guidelines, and how to contact a librarian. A public library might have a subject guide on gardening, with links to library resources as well as to local information created by the community.

Wikis have made a relatively significant impact in these areas. Because contributing to a wiki requires little technical knowledge, all librarians using wikis are in a position to edit and create their own subject guides without the aid of technology staff.

Chad Boeninger created the first business reference wiki, the Biz Wiki (see Figure 3.14). His Web site goes far beyond a typical subject guide. He includes a video introducing himself, a chat widget that allows users to talk with him in real time, and typical pages devoted to finding specific types of information. This wiki also in-

▶ Figure 3.14: Subject Guide Wiki

cludes a feed from the business blog that he also maintains. An added benefit of including all the different subject guides in the one wiki is that any business students can search across the wiki to find more information relevant to their area of study, even if their professor has not requested something specific for their class.

St. Joseph County Public Library, Indiana, has a collection of subject guides in one wiki (see Figure 3.15), as well. These subject guides deal with the local community and with ways the library can help its users.

The culture of your library will impact the openness of your wiki. You may choose to have a wiki that only a few specified people on staff can edit, or you may choose one that is open to any interested people in the community. If an open wiki makes library staff nervous, but the library staff appreciate that there is value in creating a community Web site, a possible solution is to create a club or volunteer task force that receives special training before they can update the site.

When creating a subject guide wiki, take a look at the subject guides you already produce. What information do you typically include? If you are already using video, for example, you will want to

▶ Figure 3.15: Subject Guide Wiki

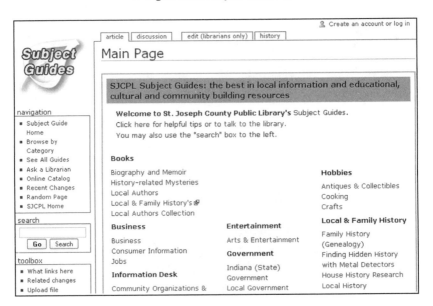

select a wiki option that will allow you to embed video. If your current guides are only text and links, any wiki will do.

As always, you will start out wanting to theme your wiki to look like your library Web site. Once your wiki is appropriately themed, you can pull content into the wiki from a few existing subject guides as a proof of concept. This is an excellent way of helping others understand your vision of the wiki as a subject guide and can be a good way to create a pilot study. If people think the idea is interesting but are not sure how your users will respond, you can do a study with users comparing and contrasting the original and wiki-based subject guides. This will help you know if a wiki is a good solution for subject guide creation in your community.

If you decide a wiki will meet your subject guide needs, you will probably want to pull over all your existing subject guides into the wiki. Patrons can become confused if there is similar information in two different places. Pulling over content will be relatively simple and most likely will require only copying and pasting content from existing documents. You might even be able to enlist student employees or volunteers to help so that library staff members do not have to spend a lot of time doing this routine work.

Once existing content has been moved to the wiki, you might want to set up a redirect so that anyone who visits the old pages is redirected to the new wiki. This will keep your patrons' bookmarks up-to-date and will minimize the advertising you will have to do to notify people of the change. You might, however, notice an increase in reference questions if people find the new format confusing. Note any increase in these questions as this will help you determine if the transition requires user education or a redesign of how the content is organized within the wiki.

Finally, you will want to work with those who create subject guides to make sure they are comfortable creating and editing them. You might want to offer classes or to sit with people who are starting out so that they see that editing the wiki is not too difficult.

How to Use Wikis for Instruction

Wikis can be used for instruction as well. Credit-bearing courses can use a wiki as a learning management system, and one-shot library instruction sessions can use a wiki to supplement classroom teaching. In either of these cases, a class wiki would include information about what you are planning to teach, information about the content, and information for students to help them with their work. Wikis are also a convenient way to provide learners with hyperlinks in lieu of a handout that would require students to type in the URLs.

Figure 3.16 shows a class wiki for an information literacy course at Wake Forest University. The wiki includes course content, information about group work, and class readings. Note that the wiki includes information to help the students use it effectively.

A course wiki could include the syllabus, lecture notes, information about projects, and collaborative spaces for students to work in. You might even create a final project that students can include in the wiki. You would want to create a framework for the class wiki before the first day so that when students come in at the beginning you can walk them through the wiki and explain how you plan to use it. You do not necessarily have to fill in all the sections, though. You can do that as the class progresses. Your students will dictate how much time you have to spend teaching the technology in the classroom. If you know your students will not be familiar with edit-

▶ Figure 3.16: Wiki for Instruction

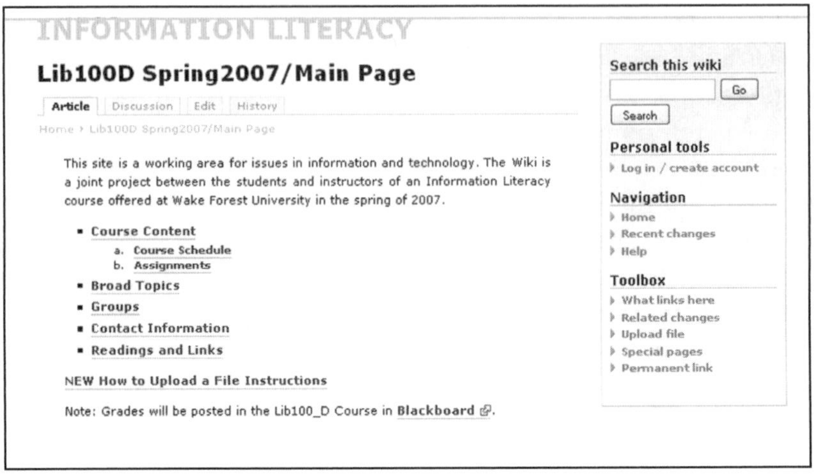

INFORMATION LITERACY

Lib100D Spring2007/Main Page

Article   Discussion   Edit   History

Home ▸ Lib100D Spring2007/Main Page

This site is a working area for issues in information and technology. The Wiki is a joint project between the students and instructors of an Information Literacy course offered at Wake Forest University in the spring of 2007.

- **Course Content**
  - a. **Course Schedule**
  - b. **Assignments**
- **Broad Topics**
- **Groups**
- **Contact Information**
- **Readings and Links**

NEW How to Upload a File Instructions

Note: Grades will be posted in the Lib100_D Course in **Blackboard** ⊡.

Search this wiki

[   ] [Go]

[Search]

Personal tools

▸ Log in / create account

Navigation

▸ Home
▸ Recent changes
▸ Help

Toolbox

▸ What links here
▸ Related changes
▸ Upload file
▸ Special pages
▸ Permanent link

ing wikis, you might choose to use a vendor hosted option with a WYSIWYG editor so that you can spend your class time on content rather than on teaching the technology. If you suspect your students are already familiar with creating online content, or one of the outcomes of the class is for them to be comfortable participating in today's information environment, you might sacrifice some class time to teach them how to edit a MediaWiki site, giving them additional skills in case they want to edit Wikipedia as they participate in class.

In the case of a one-shot session, you will probably choose to include some of the standard information that you include in subject guides. But you might also choose to incorporate instruction. If you use the wiki to teach skills such as how to perform an advanced search in the catalog or how to choose a database, you do not have to focus as much on this in class, freeing up time for critical thinking and evaluative skills training.

No matter how you incorporate a wiki into your classes, you will want to make sure students know that it is available to them. Be sure to tell them the URL and e-mail it to them. It is not worth creating the content for a wiki if your audience will never see it. Letting the reference staff know the URL for the wiki could help students who have misplaced it the night before the project is due.

Wikis are ideal solutions for many Web sites that library staff need to create in the course of library work. Because these projects are more about communicating with the users rather than about the tool that you use to create them, you will want to approach these projects the same way you would if you were using a traditional Web site. Do a needs assessment, use focus groups to find out what users want, and design the site with your users in mind. Then, behind the scenes, you can consider how to use a wiki when meeting these goals.

▶ EXPLORE OTHER WIKI USES

Conference Wikis

The American Library Association conferences have used wikis since 2005, and a growing number of conferences choose to have a wiki as their conference site or as a supplemental site for participants. These wikis often include information about travel and transportation, places to stay and roommate arrangements, information about dining and entertainment in the area, and other relevant information. Some include pages for participants to list their blog URL or Twitter username so other people can follow along with the conference activities. Some are very casual, created for and by attendees. Others are more formal, created by the conference organizers and containing official conference information (see Figure 3.17).

If you are setting up a conference wiki, begin by thinking about the purpose of the site. Is it the official Web page for the conference, or is it supplemental? Are you creating a conference site where only planners will edit the content, or is it going to be a collaborative site in which participants will be able to contribute? Does the wiki need to have a formal and official voice, or is the wiki creating a venue for the participants to share information for their own planning? Knowing how you and the conference committee feel about these questions, and what your participant's expectations are, will help you know how to design the wiki for your conference.

▶ Figure 3.17: Conference Wiki

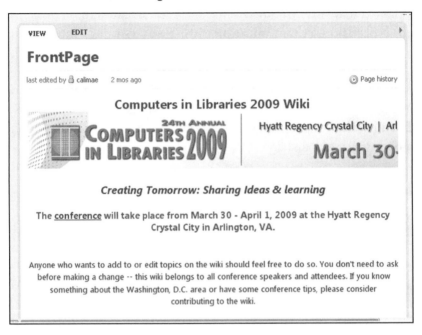

Once you have made your decisions and set up a basic framework, you will want to let participants know about the site, what they can expect to find there, and how they can participate if this is an option. You might want to seed a few sections to make the wiki worth visiting, for example, with information on local restaurants or transportation, and send out periodic e-mails pointing to the pages with the most relevant information for users at that point in time.

As is often the case, you might find that people visit the site more than they contribute, and this can be okay. It all depends on the goals and purposes of your wiki. If the purpose of the wiki is primarily to distribute information to make the conference a better experience, and secondarily about creating a community of conference goers, it is more important that people visit the site than it is for them to contribute to it, so your wiki is still a success.

Professional Resources

There are already many professional wikis for library staff and their work. These wikis can help you learn about best practices and techniques for your work, but they can also be a place for you to share what you are doing as well. These wikis can help you find the best practices for any given issue in the field as well as provide a way to connect with others who are doing work you are interested in.

Library Success Wiki
www.libsuccess.org

Library Success Wiki is designed for libraries to share what they are doing with others in the field. This list will help you find who is offering text messaging reference, new marketing ideas, and new programming ideas. The Library Success Wiki is run using MediaWiki and is primarily a best practices wiki.

Lyrasis Library Leadership Network
http://pln.palinet.org/wiki

Another professional MediaWiki site is hosted by Lyrasis, a library consortium. This wiki is the Library Leadership Network. It contains articles from people in the field dealing with leadership issues or current library news impacting the field. The site is a wiki that anyone can contribute to, but it also includes signed articles. People may modify these articles, but one of the community rules is that people will not change the meaning or message of another person's signed article.

ALA Read Write Connect
http://wikis.ala.org/readwriteconnect

ALA has a number of wikis, for everything from conferences to division wikis to wikis for specific projects. These wikis provide members with information about the organization and a place for collaborative work. These professional wikis exist both to help people with their association responsibilities and to let the library community learn about the association's work.

Contributing Original Content

In addition to professional wikis, you might consider contributing to Wikipedia on behalf of your organization. If your users turn to Wikipedia first, after all, why not put your content there? If you consider this, it would be wise to read about the culture of Wiki-pedia. Wikipedia has fundamental principles (see Pressley and McCallum, 2008, at www.infotoday.com/online/sep08/Pressley_McCallum.shtml) that guide people's contributions to the wiki:

▶ Nonmarketing

▶ Neutral point of view

▶ Verifiability

▶ No original research

When you set up an account on Wikipedia, you will need to register as an individual. Accounts that are known to belong to an organization can be deleted from the system without any warning. Once you have set up the account, you will want to follow best practices for editing Wikipedia. Of particular importance, Wikipedia does not allow individuals or groups to use the site for marketing. This includes not-for-profit organizations and libraries. Because of this, rather than adding an entry in the encyclopedia for your special collection, you might choose to add a link to your collection on a page already dealing with the topic of your collection. This way you are not using Wikipedia to pitch your library but instead including your library in the references as a place people can go to for more information.

Wikipedia does not allow original research, and you can include only information that has been documented and is verifiable. If you add a statement to an entry based on information in your collection, include a citation to the specific work. This can drive traffic to your special collections page. The citations are important. Not only do they prove you are not contributing original ideas, but they also provide verifiability to your additions. You will want to make sure you are writing with a neutral point of view. Wikipedia requires authors remove bias from their writing.

Once you have made changes to Wikipedia, you might find that they have been altered or removed after the fact. If this is the case, examine the discussion tab of your entry, the rules for editors, and the founding principles for the encyclopedia. There is a good chance that the reason your information is no longer there is because it violated Wikipedia's standards.

Making Wikipedia Better

If you have committed to editing Wikipedia to push people to your library's Web site, it is not a far stretch to approach Wikipedia editing as a professional responsibility. When you edit Wikipedia you are helping to improve one of the primary resources people turn to today. If you are interested in this work, you might want to start small with editing punctuation and formatting or contributing in spaces in which you are really comfortable. You may choose to participate in the discussion tabs to negotiate what is appropriate and relevant for a given entry.

Another way to improve Wikipedia for your users is to incorporate Context Objects in Spans, or COinS. COinS is a specific way of citing a source on a Web site, and it is integrated into Wikipedia. With a browser plug-in, and a click of a button, users can see links to full-text options for works cited with COinS. Figure 3.18 shows how the COinS displays in the browser. Users can click on the "Full Text Options" link to be redirected to a library site with the full text of the articles.

▶ Figure 3.18: COinS

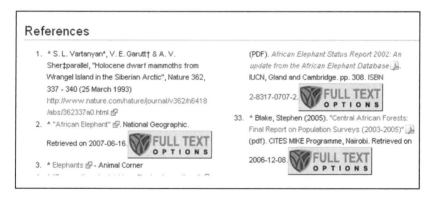

▶4

MARKETING

- ▶ **Get the Word Out**
- ▶ **Market to the Intended Audience**
- ▶ **Advertise via Social Media**
- ▶ **Create a Marketing Plan**

A Web site is only useful if it is relevant and used by its intended audience. A wiki is no different. You can spend hours planning and setting up a wiki, but if no one visits your site or it does not include information users find valuable, then all your wiki efforts will be in vain.

This chapter addresses ways that you can market your wiki and help create an audience base to sustain it over time. Your strategy will depend on whether the wiki is designed for internal or external use. The initiator of the wiki will also impact your marketing strategy. If the administration initiates the wiki, your marketing strategy will be very different from marketing a wiki that was initiated by the larger community. This section will provide you with the tools necessary to plan a marketing strategy for your new wiki.

▶ GET THE WORD OUT

When you start thinking about marketing your wiki, you will want to consider who it is for. This information can help you craft a marketing plan for your specific audience. For example, if administration would like the staff to use a wiki, but the staff had not indicated an interest in the site, you might need to call on the administration to offer rewards for participation or some other incentive. However, if your patrons have requested a community wiki, you can begin your marketing plan with your patron's word-of-mouth advertising. Incentives and word-of-mouth advertising won't be your entire marketing plan, but they can be a component of your plan. You should consider using a number of approaches, including prominent location on your Web site, special meetings or programming, publications or flyers, and one-on-one sessions with interested users. This section will address these methods in more detail.

Location on the Library Web Site

As part of your marketing plan, you will want to consider what role you wiki has on the main library's Web site. Is the wiki easy to find? You will want to consider how prominently you would like the wiki to be displayed on your Web site, and the location will probably change over time. For example, when the wiki is new, you might want to make sure it is more visible as part of the kick-off campaign. Once the wiki is more established you might choose to reserve the most prominent space for new programs.

You will want to link the wiki in the appropriate place on the Web site. If you are using the wiki to provide subject guides, you will want to put it in the research section. If you want the wiki to provide answers to frequently asked questions, you might want the wiki to replace that section of the Web site.

If the wiki is for library staff only, you may choose to keep the wiki in a less prominent area of the site, or you may choose not to link to the wiki at all. In this case you would want to make sure to market the wiki's address prominently to staff through e-mail and maybe even on paper so that they will be able to find it despite the lack of a link on the library's homepage.

Programming

Another effective marketing technique is to offer programming related to the wiki for its intended audience. This programming can focus on what the purpose of the wiki is and on how one can use it to make life easier. You can also offer an instructional program on how to edit and participate in the wiki.

When planning your program, be guided by the reason the wiki exists and by who the primary users are. Perhaps for a group of teens you could create a game in which, over the course of a month, the teen who contributes the most content gets a prize or recognition on the front page of the wiki. For an adult book club you might consider having a meeting to which everyone brings their favorite book and walks through the steps of adding an entry on their favorite book to the wiki.

The programming, of course, will be structured differently depending on if your audience is your community or your library staff. Wiki programs could be offered along the same lines as other community programs. A program could be part of your regular schedule for any user interested in the topic or the technology. If you are working on a wiki for library staff, the training could be rolled into staff meetings or integrated into the library staff training program.

Flyers/Publications

In all likelihood, your library already has a system for communicating with your users. You can make use of this system to market your wiki as well. If you distribute a newsletter, it makes sense to highlight what the wiki offers in an article introducing the new site. If you send out regular e-mails whenever there is something newsworthy, you may choose to send an e-mail announcing your new wiki. If you are already using blogs, you might even offer a series of posts on what the wiki is and how to use it.

It does not hurt to market your wiki in public places as well. You can post flyers around your building letting people know specific features that might make their lives easier. You might choose to post flyers in more public spaces reminding people of the library and highlighting the wiki as a new service that you are offering the community.

If you have a person, or committee, on staff that is responsible for this type of marketing, it certainly makes sense to see what recommendations they have and to empower them to market the wiki as well.

One-on-One Sessions

You might also find yourself in settings where you can introduce individuals to your wiki one-on-one. These are excellent opportunities to teach a user how to interact with the wiki and also to get a sense of where the wiki could be clearer, easier to use, or reorganized. Once you have successfully worked with a user, that individual might even develop enough interest to talk about the wiki with other library users, encouraging others through word-of-mouth advertising.

▶ MARKET TO THE INTENDED AUDIENCE

The question of your audience is an important one. Your approach will vary depending on if your audience is your users or your fellow library staff members. If your wiki is designed for public use, you are marketing to a broad base of people with a broad level of technology skills. Some of your users might be familiar with wikis and edit Wikipedia. Others will not be able to distinguish your wiki site from any other type of Web site. You may choose to create marketing plans for people at different comfort

---

Technology Skill Levels and Wiki Use

Novice:
- ▶ Use the search box
- ▶ Cut and paste
- ▶ Embed links
- ▶ Know terms such as "wiki"

Intermediate:
- ▶ Embed media
- ▶ Plug in widgets
- ▶ Create new pages
- ▶ Know terms such as "history" or "discussion tabs"

Advanced:
- ▶ Use extensions
- ▶ Add CoinS
- ▶ Know terms such as "hosting" and "extensions"

levels with the technology. For those who are really technologically advanced, you might create programming focused on how to enhance the wiki to make it more useful. For those with less experience, you might choose to emphasize that the Web site exists and teach users how to find information on it.

These approaches might work well for staff as well, but you can also make different assumptions about a wiki created for library staff. For example, if administration requires that all library staff use the wiki as a centralized repository for information about the running of the library, everyone will need to be able to use and edit the wiki. You might still have to plan programming and documentation for people across the spectrum, but you can assume everyone will need to gain the same level of competency.

External Strategies

We have talked a little about how marketing and training might vary based on audience, so let us go into strategy a little bit deeper for both internal and external marketing. Marketing a wiki to an external audience is similar to anything you might market to your users. You might choose to post flyers and signs around your library or distribute bookmarks with the wiki's URL. You may set the screen on the library computers to the wiki as a way to make sure all computer users see the wiki at least once. Your marketing strategy for the community should be focused on how the wiki could help them out.

Although the wiki is on the computer, you can use the launch as an excuse to get out into the community. You can have a launch party at the mall for teens or partner with local businesses. You could set up a table in a grocery store to show people how to add cooking tips or information about local foods. This might increase interest in the community and give people a reason to come back and visit other sections of the wiki.

Internal Strategies

Your biggest influence on strategy for an internal wiki is the initiator of the wiki. If management requires the wiki, you can count on people learning what they need to know to participate in the use of the wiki as part of their jobs, but there might be more initial resistance to a new wiki as well. You might need to get a statement from administration requiring that everyone contribute one piece of information or offering incentives for those who make a contribution.

Marketing the Idea Behind the Wiki

Many people today recognize the importance of an organization's Web presence. Some even understand how to make use of social software and Web sites like blogs, Facebook, or Twitter. Though Wikis are part of this type of technology, they are not understood by as many people. When speaking with stakeholders and staff members, it will be important for you to explain the purpose of your Web site and to define "wiki" in a way that is meaningful to them. You will also want to describe how a wiki will enable you to better meet users' needs and to accomplish your goals.

If the wiki is a grassroots product, you will not need as many incentives, but you may have to spend more time making sure everyone is on board—not just the subset of people who requested it. In this case you might have to convince the administrators to support the project and teach them exactly what a wiki is and how it can be helpful. When getting people on board early, you should talk with your technology staff from the very beginning! These staff members know your technical system best and will help you avoid software that's not compatible with your current system or choosing an outdated product. If you can get their buy-in at an early phase, they will be more invested in your project and have their own incentive to work on it.

As discussed in Chapter 3, initiating a wiki requires seeding the wiki with relevant information. You will want to have enough information to make it worth your colleagues' time to visit it. If there is not enough information in the wiki, your colleagues will not use the site. If they do not use the wiki, they will not add content. If you seed the wiki with information, and people find it useful, they will begin marketing the wiki for you by letting others know about the information available. As they become more familiar with the wiki they will also be more comfortable contributing their own content.

Perhaps the most effective strategy for working with staff is to let people know how to get help. This help could be programming, handouts, one-on-one training, or even a buddy system whereby staff members pair up to make changes. If people know they can get the help they need—easily and quickly—they will be more willing to take a chance contributing.

▶ ADVERTISE VIA SOCIAL MEDIA

Today we also have new media options for marketing products, including other wikis. The users who are on Facebook and Twitter and who blog are also probably going to be your primary candidates for early wiki adoption. If you are marketing the wiki to an external audience it makes sense to look into marketing in these places. You can buy advertisements fairly cheaply through Facebook and target them to specific demographics such as your students or people who live in your ZIP code. You can write about your wiki in blogs, and you can leave comments about your wiki on others' blogs. Please note that some bloggers might perceive self-promotional comments as spam, so it is important to consider if your comment is appropriate.

You can also make media for people to add to their own sites to market your wiki. You can make a small badge or logo to link to

Google AdWords

Google AdWords is a way of marketing your public wiki through Google. The text ads you see at the top or the right of a search are generated using the AdWords system. To participate, you begin by selecting relevant keywords. When users search Google with these keywords, your site comes up in the search as an advertisement. Costs vary; http://adwords.google.com can provide you with an estimate of how much a particular string of keywords would cost based on keyword traffic. You set a daily amount that you are willing to spend, and how much you are willing to spend per click, and you will not be charged beyond that.

your wiki that fans can put on their own Web sites. You can make short videos or screencasts of your wiki and share them on media Web sites like YouTube and Vimeo. There are a number of relevant social media sites with users who are good candidates for working with wikis. Use this to your advantage and market with them!

▶ CREATE A MARKETING PLAN

Your total marketing strategy will be based on the purpose of the wiki, the group or people who requested it, and the state of the wiki at the point when you begin marketing it. Once you have a clear understanding of your wiki, its audience, and its context, you can create an effective plan. You will want to consider its placement on the Web site, the training and programming you will offer, advertisements in publications and other media, and what forms of help you will provide to those who need it. A holistic approach to marketing will allow you to share your wiki with a wide audience of people who will benefit from its creation.

▶5

BEST PRACTICES

▶ **Know How to Plan**

▶ **Outline the Implementation Steps**

▶ **Strategize Marketing**

▶ **Maintain Your Wiki**

▶ **Keep Your Software Current and Have a Preservation Plan**

No matter the type of wiki you are using, or the way you intend to use it, there are a number of concepts that are useful across the board. When implementing a wiki you will want to have strong plans in place for a number of areas:

▶ An assessment to understand the context of the wiki and its audience

▶ A rollout plan for introducing the wiki to its audience

▶ A training plan for those who will use and edit the wiki

▶ A marketing plan for advertising the wiki

▶ A maintenance plan for keeping the wiki current and up-to-date

▶ A migration plan in case you choose to move the wiki at a later date

▶ A preservation plan in case your vendor stops offering the wiki service or if you plan to take down the wiki at a later point

This chapter will discuss some of the essential practices for using wikis in libraries.

► KNOW HOW TO PLAN

When designing your wiki, you will want to spend some time in the planning stages, making sure that you have thought through the objectives of the wiki, how you will use it, as well as how you will get others on board and establish its place within your library. The planning stage is behind the scenes but extremely important. This is the phase during which you will lay the groundwork for what you are trying to do. The work in this phase can be really exciting, as you are experimenting with new ideas and ways of doing things, but it may also be less engaging because you will not immediately see the outcome of the work that you are doing. Keep these questions in mind during the planning phase:

1. What are the goals and expected outcomes of your wiki?
2. How will this wiki make your library's work easier or of a better quality?
3. What tools and widgets make the most sense given the goals, functional expectations, and technological expectations of your place of work?
4. Who will be responsible for the wiki?
5. What is your plan for seeding the wiki?
6. How do you plan to train others to participate?
7. How will you determine if the use of the wiki was a success?

Spending time thinking through and answering these questions will help you formulate your plan for the use of the wiki and will help ensure that the wiki is a success. If you are planning a very small pilot project to get a feel for how a wiki might work for you in your workplace, you may want to read through these questions a number of times as you experiment to remind yourself of what to look for. There are times for pure experimentation and times for clear and thorough planning, and the amount of preplanning you do depends on where you are in this process.

► OUTLINE THE IMPLEMENTATION STEPS

A strong rollout of your wiki is the foundation for a good implementation process. Good wiki implementation includes creating an outline of the information you anticipate adding to the wiki, what information you will seed it with, details of your training program, and details of your marketing plan.

When creating the basic outline of the wiki, you are creating the container in which people will add information. You will want to think through how people would want information organized. You will probably need to have conversations with various stakeholders to ensure that you are making something that will be useful to everyone.

There are, of course, a few basic ways people can think about this. If you are creating a library wiki, you might want to create a page for each department and let the department staff figure out how to organize the information in a structure relevant to them. If your wiki is for an event, you will want a page for the who, what, where, when, and why of the event. If you are not sure about how to get started organizing your wiki, you can take a look at any number of library wikis out there to see how others have organized theirs.

At this point, you might guess that another very important part of implementation is seeding the wiki with relevant information. This comes up again and again because it is so important to the

Seeding Your Wiki

Seeding the wiki depends on the use you envision for your wiki. If it is going to be a reference source for how the library works, you might create a section for each department. For example, you might choose to have sections of the wiki devoted to reference, circulation, children's services, technical services, technology, and administration. If you are planning to use a wiki to collaborate on a specific project, you might create sections to deal with an overview of your goals and deadlines, background information, task lists, and contact information for all involved parties. Based on the intended use for your wiki, you can create the basic outline for the information that will be contained and begin the overview text for each section. Over time, as the project or resource develops, the community can refine the organizational structure and information contained within the site.

success of your wiki. If you do not have good information in the wiki to start with, people will not have any reason to visit it. You should plan to add as much information as you possibly can during the implementation phase. Do you have manuals stored digitally that you can copy and paste into the wiki? Do you have e-mails that contain instructions for how to perform specific tasks? Any existing documentation is a good candidate for copying and pasting into the wiki. If you do not have access to existing files, or if you do not know enough to populate the wiki yourself, it is time to enlist the help of others who might be able to contribute. You might choose to turn to a representative from each department if you are in a larger library. Getting participation from a wide variety of people in your library will help you once you are marketing the wiki and trying to encourage its use.

While in the implementation phase, you will want to decide how to approach training. As we have discussed, you should include a variety of approaches to training. Consider choosing a hybrid approach of at least some of the following:

- ▶ Face-to-face classes
- ▶ One-on-one training
- ▶ Online tutorials
- ▶ "Cheat sheet" worksheets
- ▶ An "on call" system with someone who is willing to help

Once you've figured out the structure of the wiki, included some introductory information, and decided how you will approach training, you will be ready to roll out the wiki. And when you do this, it is time to increase your marketing activities.

▶ STRATEGIZE MARKETING

As discussed in Chapter 5, marketing is a core part of getting your wiki out there and in use by its audience. We discussed several ways of marketing in Chapter 5:

- ▶ Post flyers and signage.
- ▶ Create bookmarks and takeaways.

▶ Place the wiki prominently on your Web site.

▶ Offer a training program.

▶ Run related programs.

▶ Use the wiki as the homepage on library computers.

▶ Use social networking and Web 2.0 sites.

▶ Target a few key players who can influence others.

When thinking about marketing it is always important to think about who your audience is and what they can get from the wiki. Will it be just another source of information for them, or will it be a social networking opportunity? How would this wiki fit into their day-to-day lives? Is there any aspect of it that will make their lives easier? Understanding your users, and how the wiki will be useful for them, is an excellent starting place for developing your marketing plan. That marketing plan will guide the advertising you do for the wiki and ultimately the use and success of the project. Start with where your users are, and you will be able to make good inroads.

▶ MAINTAIN YOUR WIKI

After you have planned the wiki, implemented it, and marketed it to others, the wiki becomes a living Web site. Others are editing and contributing, and you are stepping away from individual ownership. At this point, it is worth thinking about maintenance.

It is easy for people to add information to a wiki, once they know how. It is generally easy for users to remember to add information when something new happens, a policy is changed, or there is a new frequently asked question. However, some information in the wiki might become outdated because no one thinks about checking up on it. In a large organization, this could be less of an issue. A larger audience has more potential for catching errors in the wiki. However, mistakes might slip through the cracks even in a large organization. It is a good idea to have a few designated people check designated sections of the wiki on a regular basis. Your organization might do this when it checks the library Web site for out-of-date information or dead links.

Your staff might include one or two people who really enjoy working with the wiki, who would not mind going through and tagging pages that seem to be out of date or incomplete. These editors could follow up by sending an e-mail to the people who have the newer information and can update the pages. This is the perfect task to fill those last few hours before a conference or a slow shift at the reference desk. The goal at this point is to make sure that the old and out-of-date information is removed from the wiki so that people can rely on the wiki to be accurate and up-to-date.

▶ KEEP YOUR SOFTWARE CURRENT AND HAVE A PRESERVATION PLAN

Finally, you will want a plan for the life span of your wiki. This is less of an issue for vendor hosted wikis. However, you will have to check for software updates periodically for those on your own server and then update the wiki when a new version is released. This could become difficult if you are hosting a large number of wikis or if your technology staff is already pressed for time.

If you know that a wiki will be relevant only for a given amount of time, you will want to plan an archival method so that the information is not lost. This way you will not need to keep updating the wiki software, but you will be able to continue providing the information to those who were interested in the topic.

If you plan to keep the wiki for a long period of time, you will want to pay attention to the software and the hosting company to ensure that the software is still current and good. If you can tell that the company is about to go out of business, or if you would like to switch to a locally hosted option, you will want to make sure that you can easily convert the information between the two wiki platforms.

This will vary depending on the wiki platform that you are leaving and the one you are beginning to use. If there is not an easy way to export and import your wiki's data, you will need to pull the content out of your first wiki and enter it into the second one manually. A volunteer or student, depending on the sensitivity of the information and responsibility of the individual, can do this work.

Tips for Converting Your Wiki

1. Learn the syntax for the new wiki. How do internal and external links work? How does this compare to the first wiki?
2. Copy the basic organizational structure from the first wiki and paste it into the new wiki. Edit the syntax so internal pages are created.
3. One page at a time, copy content from the original wiki, and put the content in the new one, editing syntax as you go. As you do this, you can delete the pages from the original wiki.
4. Once you have made significant progress, you can access the list of pages for the original wiki to make sure you are not missing any in the conversion process.

▶6

MEASURES OF SUCCESS

- ▶ **People Use the Wiki to Look for Information**
- ▶ **People Add Information to the Wiki**
- ▶ **People Are Aware of the Wiki**
- ▶ **People Initiate Other Wikis**
- ▶ **The Wiki Is Part of Library Culture**

Wiki adoption can be slow. Although wikis can help organizations in a number of ways, sometimes people are hesitant to integrate them into their daily work. People may be reluctant for a number of reasons. Perhaps people prefer to avoid new technologies. It might be difficult to change a workflow pattern after a tradition of accomplishing tasks a specific way. Perhaps people do not understand why the wiki has been introduced to the organization. It is worth monitoring the use of your new wiki with any of its intended audiences to get a sense of how people are feeling about the site and if they have any hesitations. If they do, you can create training and target marketing to alleviate them. If users have a discomfort with the tool, you might want to offer more training or one-on-one help. If the problem is workflow, you could work with administration to see if there is a way to relieve staff of some duties while they develop their new workflow processes.

It is worth noting that, although wiki adoption can be slow, as long as you see the adoption moving in a positive direction, then it is likely that the adoption is progressing well. The dynamics of wiki adoption change over time, often starting with acceptance and use by a small group and then moving toward a general adoption. One person can begin to build the interest and use of a wiki and then

Survey Questions to Consider

Question	Rationale
What led you to this Web site?	This will let you know if people are coming to the Web site because they know about it or if they are coming to it through an Internet search.
What information were you seeking?	With this information, you can learn what information people need, and what sections of the wiki you might enhance.
Did you find the answers you needed?	This will let you know if the information was in-depth enough or if you need to add more content.
Would you recommend this Web site to others in the future?	You will learn if you need to make large changes to meet users' needs and if you can count on word-of-mouth marketing.
Would you be willing to participate in a focus group on our Web site? If so, please leave your contact information.	The best feedback you can get on the usefulness of your wiki comes from your users. Focus groups allow you to have conversations about your wiki, its organization, the content, and other variables that might impact the usefulness of the wiki.

win over others one by one. If you don't want to wait for a slow adoption, there are some techniques you can consider to get people on board more quickly:

▶ Be sure your new wiki starts out with enough information to be useful.

▶ Monitor the information in your wiki to ensure it is accurate, and check up on it periodically.

▶ Enlist a few people to be early adopters, and reward your first editors for their participation.

▶ Monitor e-mail discussion lists. When questions arise, post the answer in the wiki and reply with a link to the page with the answer.

▶ PEOPLE USE THE WIKI TO LOOK FOR INFORMATION

For the wiki to be useful for the community, the community needs to know they can look there for information. To educate them, you have to do a few things: make sure there is enough useful information in the wiki for your community to find it relevant, market the wiki well so that people know how to find it, and make it easy to use so that your users will find the information that they look for.

We have talked about these issues in previous chapters, but if you find yourself wondering why people are not looking in the wiki and are turning to other sources, these could be issues. Consider the usefulness of your wiki. Does the wiki have information in it that you would look for yourself? Is the site organized in a way in which you can find what you need? Ask others if they find the wiki useful and what improvements they might suggest. If people agree that the wiki is generally useful, perhaps you should look into how you marketed the wiki. If your users visit the library Web site, can they easily find the wiki? Do you mention it in other online places where people regularly visit? Have you sent out e-mail reminders when people ask about information that you know to be in the wiki? You need to explore a variety of different factors when trying to determine where the marketing is not working.

▶ PEOPLE ADD INFORMATION TO THE WIKI

A sign that your wiki is working is the growth of the site. If people find the wiki valuable they will participate, and the wiki will continue to grow and become more valuable over time. If you find that the wiki is not growing, or that you are the only one contributing, it is worth exploring how to make the wiki a friendlier site to use. Perhaps you find that people do access the wiki but are not adding information as regularly or consistently as you had hoped. In this case, perhaps the interface is not as intuitive as you had thought or perhaps the staff need a second round of training.

If you want to get people to add more content, you might find value in revisiting Chapter 3 on implementation for specific suggestions. In general, however, make sure that it is easy for people to add content, and provide plenty of educational opportunities. You can offer one-on-one training, workshops, or online instructional videos to help. If you are looking to create a feeling of ownership in the wiki's audience, you could agree to add others' information for them for a specified period of time.

Helpful Online Instructional Videos

To get a sense of the tone, styles, and type of information people convey in online instructional videos, take a look at the following. You might even find that some already answer the questions you know your community members have, and you can send the link to them as a response.

- ▶ Getting Started with PBWiki (now PBworks): www.youtube.com/watch?v=A2O4JcGQiY0
- ▶ WetPaint in Plain English: www.youtube.com/watch?v=F7BAU2XX5Ws
- ▶ Wiki Basic Editing Tips: www.youtube.com/watch?v=xvLIR1FbC2Y
- ▶ Editing a Wiki: www.youtube.com/watch?v=bH15MEfOJRY
- ▶ Creating and Editing a Wiki Page: www.youtube.com/watch?v=0S9KQS-twFU
- ▶ Add and Edit a Page in MediaWiki: www.youtube.com/watch?v=6gbMNhnl1SU
- ▶ Introduction to a Class Wiki: www.youtube.com/watch?v=6NRbbskf3cA

▶▶ PEOPLE ARE AWARE OF THE WIKI

Another way that you can know that the wiki is going well is if people seem more aware of what is going on or at least more aware of how to find out what is going on. When there is a general sense that the information is findable, especially since the launch of the wiki, you can assume that it is playing a role in the community. You will know this for certain if you see others responding to questions by pointing to the wiki.

Again, by monitoring library discussion lists, you will get an idea of how people are responding to the wiki. Are there more, the same, or fewer requests for information? When people send information to the discussion list, do they also post it to the wiki? How active is your listserv? If you are not sure, you can look through the archives, comparing the same month or even week over a couple years.

If you have not noticed a change in people's awareness, revisit the marketing and training chapters of this book. You might also want to contribute more information to the wiki so that people know to look there first. Perhaps enlist a few others to add content as well. This will create a core group of people to recommend the wiki when people ask questions. Hopefully these additional voices will also help your audience learn where the wiki is, why it is useful, and how to participate.

▶ PEOPLE INITIATE OTHER WIKIS

You will know that the wiki is a success if you find that people are creating new sections in the wiki for their own committee or departmental use or if they are creating their own wikis for specific projects or events. This is a sign that others see the value of the tool and have learned ways that a wiki can improve their own work.

This adoption might take a while, and it could benefit from reminders along the way. People may not think of their own use for a wiki, but, after learning how one works and hearing other ideas, they might become interested in trying to establish one on their own. If you would like to support this type of adaptation, be willing to share some of the ideas mentioned in this book and other tips that you learn along the way. Truly, wikis are helpful in many contexts; it is just a matter of thinking through what would be most helpful in a given area.

▶ THE WIKI IS PART OF LIBRARY CULTURE

The clearest indicator that the wiki is successful is when it is no longer your own project. At some point, a successful wiki will become part of the library's culture. Others might even tend to the project more than you do. The introduction of wikis has been successful when you are no longer the primary source of information on the topic and the general institutional culture expects people to be comfortable with the tool.

This transition may feel strange at first—losing authority over a tool that you introduced to the culture. However, it is good for the organization. It is an indication that the wiki is now a core part of the library culture and is a foundation for the work the library does. If you can get your organization to this point, your wiki is a success.

RECOMMENDED READING

▶ BOOKS

Klobas, Jane E. and Angela Beesley. 2006. *Wikis: Tools for Information Work and Collaboration.* Oxford: Chandos.

Shirky, Clay. 2008. *Here Comes Everybody: The Power of Organizing Without Organizations.* New York: Penguin Press.

Tapscott, Don and Anthony D. Williams. 2006. *Wikinomics: How Mass Collaboration Changes Everything.* New York: Portfolio.

▶ CHAPTERS

Casey, Michael. 2007. "The Wonderful World of Wikis: Applications for Libraries." In *Library 2.0 and Beyond: Innovative Technologies and Tomorrow's User,* edited by Nancy Courtney. Westport, CT: Libraries Unlimited.

Farkas, Meredith G. 2007. "Wikis." In *Social Software in Libraries: Building Collaboration, Communication, and Community Online.* Medford, NJ: Information Today.

Kroski, Ellyssa. 2008. "Wikis." In *Web 2.0 for Librarians and Information Professionals.* New York: Neal-Schuman.

Russell, John. 2008. "Wikis and Collaborative Reference Services." In *The Desk and Beyond: Next Generation Reference Services,* edited by Sarah K. Steiner and M. Leslie Madden. Chicago: Association of College and Research Libraries.

▶ WEB SITES

ALA Read Write Connect. Available: http://wikis.ala.org/read writeconnect/index.php/Main_Page (accessed December 14, 2009).

Library Success: A Best Practices Wiki. Available: www.libsuccess .org/index.php?title=Main_Page (accessed December 14, 2009).

Lyrasis Library Leadership Network. Available: http://pln.palinet .org/wiki/index.php/LLN_Home (accessed December 14, 2009).

MediaWiki Handbook. Available: http://meta.wikimedia.org/ wiki/Help:Contents (accessed December 14, 2009).

WikiMatrix: Compare Them All. Available: www.wikimatrix.org (accessed December 14, 2009).

▶ CITED ARTICLES

Giles, Jim. 2005. "Special Report: Internet Encyclopedias Go Head to Head." *Nature* 438 (December). Available: www.nature.com/ nature/journal/v438/n7070/full/438900a.html (accessed December 14, 2009).

Pressley, Lauren and Carolyn McCallum. 2008. "Putting the Library in Wikipedia." *Online* 32, no. 5 (September/October). Available: www.infotoday.com/online/sep08/Pressley_McCallum .shtml (accessed December 14, 2009).

INDEX

Page numbers followed by the letter "f" indicate figures.

ABOUT THE AUTHOR

Lauren Pressley is the Instructional Design Librarian at Wake Forest University. She holds a BA degree in Philosophy and Communication from North Carolina State University and an MLIS from the University of North Carolina–Greensboro. She is active in the American Library Association, Library and Information Technology Association, and the Association of College and Research Libraries, and she regularly presents and writes on issues relating to education and technology in libraries. She was a member of the 2008 ALA Emerging Leaders class. In 2009, she was named a *Library Journal* Mover & Shaker. Lauren's first book, *So You Want to Be a Librarian*, was published in 2009 by Library Juice Press. More information can be found on her Web site at www.laurenpressley .com.

UNIVERSITY OF MAINE AT AUGUSTA

3 2304 00092263 1

JUN   8 2010